The Personal Workbook
for
Breaking the Chain
of
Low Self-Esteem:

A Proven Program for Recovery from LSE

Marilyn J. Sorensen, Ph.D.

Wolf Publishing Co.
Sherwood, OR 97140

2002 The Personal Workbook for Breaking the Chain of Low Self-Esteem:
A Proven Program for Recovery from LSE

Copyright 2002 by Marilyn J. Sorensen, Ph.D.
mjsorensen@TheSelfEsteemInstitute.com
Wolf Publishing Co.
16890 SW Daffodil St.
Sherwood, OR 97140
Phone or Fax: 503-925-8806
Website: www.TheSelfEsteemInstitute.com

Library of Congress Control Number: 2002092474

10   9   8   7   6   5   4   3   2   1

ISBN: 09664315-3-7
Printed in the United States

Editor: Jill Kelly, Ph.D.
Cover design and layout: Anita Jones, Another Jones Graphics
Photo by Cindy George-Whitehead

Contents

Acknowledgments

My sincere thanks to Dr. Jill Kelly, my amazing editor, whose work is unsurpassed.

Thanks also to the many clients I have had the privilege of working with and whose recovery has encouraged me in the development of this program.

Dedication

To the growing number of counselors, teachers, therapists, psychologists, and psychiatrists who recognize the seriousness of low self-esteem, who view it as a valid disorder rather than merely a symptom, and who desire to equip themselves to meet the needs of the millions of LSE sufferers who now go mistreated, overmedicated, and misdiagnosed.

P r e f a c e

Hundreds of readers who read my first book, **Breaking the Chain of Low Self-Esteem,** have written, phoned, or emailed me to say thanks and to say how the book felt like a diary of their own lives. Many said they had devoured every self-help book they could get their hands on but had not found anything that so closely mirrored their experience nor so thoroughly explained what low self-esteem (LSE) is and how it works to negatively control and distort their thinking process. Some said they cried through much of it because it resurrected painful buried memories. Some said they read it again and again; some said they wondered how I could know them so well without ever having met them.

Among these responses were many from people who had no idea that low self-esteem was the culprit that had created the havoc in their lives. After spending many hours with one or more therapists and after paying hundreds, even thousands of dollars for therapy, they claimed they had felt no closer to an answer than when they began to seek help. Others said they had gotten some help in therapy, but that their lives hadn't really changed; they still grappled with the same problems and disappointments. Then, upon *reading* **Breaking the Chain of Low Self-Esteem,** these same readers said a light bulb turned on for them—that for the first time, they saw themselves—their unfulfilled lives, their discarded dreams, their distorted thinking, and their self-sabotaging behaviors—crystal clear.

Some of these readers said that the book changed their lives, rescued failing relationships, or at least got them moving in the right direction. Many, however, said that with their thorough understanding of their self-defeating behavior and a start toward recovery, they wanted more guidance, that they needed more help to break their long-standing cycles of self-defeating behaviors and negative thinking.

This workbook is my response to the many requests for more direction. This workbook is a companion to **Breaking the Chain...** While there is no way to duplicate in writing the work I do with an individual in therapy, I have attempted to provide here a similar experience with the exercises and directions that the LSE sufferer participating in my proven program of recovery would do. Like therapy in my office, this workbook focuses entirely on the core issues that accompany LSE, rather than on the symptoms.

Is This Workbook for You?

This workbook, a companion to the book, ***Breaking the Chain of Low Self-Esteem*** (1998), is designed to guide you in your recovery from low self-esteem. Don't be misled by society's view of this problem. Low self-esteem is a serious issue that controls and thus negatively affects the lives of millions of people. Unlike the simplistic view that people often have of low self-esteem, the truth is that LSE is a complex problem and one not easily overcome. But *recovery is possible.*

By now, if you are one of the people who suffers from this problem, you know that a person doesn't just "get over it," as you may have been told to do, nor does it eventually go away, even though there may be times when your life is going well and your self-esteem issues seem to recede. While you may not always be in the throes of LSE, you know from your own experience that the self-doubts are still there. Though they may be temporarily buried, they are waiting to raise their ugly heads. If you have been in therapy one or more times and have been urged to take medication, you may also know that medication is not a way of overcoming low self-esteem; rather, it is merely a means of relieving some of the symptoms and then only for as long as you stay on the medication.

Most books and programs that claim to offer solutions for self-esteem issues are designed to help people "improve" their self-esteem and as such, these programs apply to everyone, since most people at times feel their self-esteem could stand improvement. Yet, these programs focus on altering self-defeating behavior through exercises that do not get at the core of the problem: the lifelong patterns and consequences of irrational thinking.

This book, however, is very different. It is based on a method proven to provide lasting results and is written specifically for those who have low self-esteem and who need a recovery method the goal of which is to alter their entire thinking process. This is not a program that simply involves learning new communication or assertiveness skills. Rather this is a program that:

1. **Delves directly to the root of low self-esteem**

2. **Directs those with LSE to analyze and pinpoint the unhealthy sources in his background**

3. Clarifies how these unhealthy people create LSE in young people by their inappropriate behavior and distorted messages

4. Explains the irrational and faulty thinking that evolves from this inappropriate behavior and these distorted messages

5. Illustrates how feelings are the result of thinking, not the other way around as most people believe

5. Illuminates the tumultuous emotions and self-sabotaging behaviors that evolve from faulty thinking

6. Spells out the need for a long-term recovery program in which a person's videotape must be edited and rewritten

7. Provides a reliable roadmap to reprogramming the LSE sufferer's thinking so that it is based solely on truth, fact, and the person's historical record

Therefore, if you suffer from low self-esteem, not just occasional discontent, and you are motivated to overcome this problem, **this workbook is for you.**

Low self-esteem, which forms in childhood, can be defined as a negative and distorted view of self. LSE becomes solidified over a period of years, partly from our own doing. In the beginning, we are given messages by word or deed that indicate we are inadequate; then, believing what we have been told, we pick up the ball and run with it by continuing to promote this negative self-view *of* ourselves *to* ourselves, thus cementing our belief in our inadequacy. Whether you are 23, 38, 45, 57, or 69, you most probably have expertly maintained your negative self-talk over that whole time. Consequently, it's reasonable to expect that countering the *millions* of self-delivered negative messages and breaking the habit of viewing yourself in a negative light will be a difficult task. Indeed, the road to recovery from LSE is a lengthy and often arduous one. This reality is not intended to discourage you or to weed out the faint of heart; rather it is to keep you from expecting for a quick fix and to avoid misleading you into believing that this will be an easy trek. For this journey of recovery will be a pilgrimage to a foreign way of thinking, of understanding your past, of viewing the present and, most importantly, of reshaping what otherwise might be an unfulfilling future.

If you have taken the questionnaire at the end of Chapter 1 of **Breaking the Chain of Low Self-Esteem,** you now know the severity of your low self-esteem. If you have not yet taken it, or if you still question whether you have LSE, take the questionnaire before proceeding. In all likelihood, however, because you have picked up this book, you already know that you struggle with this problem or you are close to someone who does. If it's you who needs to work through the recovery process, this journey is one you will want to commit to, remembering that your LSE will stay with you until you decide to overcome it.

At times this expedition will reveal new insights to you, which may result in exhilarating emotions; at other points, the repetition of practice to improve skills and alter dysfunctional patterns may seem boring and tedious. One week you may feel you are making great progress, the next week you may have doubts. When this happens, remember that this is to be expected: as with any new skill, progress and mastery seem to go back and forth, with good days and bad days, with good weeks and bad weeks. Eventually, however, with determined and steady practice, you will develop more expertise in wielding your new skill with more consistency. For example, most of us have learned to drive an automobile, yet when we first drove into a big city or over a mountain, we might have felt a bit shaky about driving in unfamiliar terrain. Similarly, we may feel comfortable using our computers at home but might find when taking a computer class, that our skills are insufficient for us to keep up with the instructions and exercises being presented by the teacher—at least until our skills become more extensive. There is also the plateau effect when learning new skills. We often learn the basics but have to work much harder to improve from a minimal skill level to that of being able to use the skill in new circumstances or when tested.

Additionally, many other factors may enter into how successful you feel your recovery progress is. For instance, as you begin to work on controlling your negative thinking, you may perceive that you are doing well in one setting but later feel that you failed in another situation that was more personal or that you deemed more important, or that was unexpected. Be patient with yourself; in time you will be able to generalize from one situation to another and apply your new skills across a broader spectrum.

During the stages of discovery, you may experience fear and pain; long-forgotten and hurtful memories may reappear. You may experience moments of sadness over time wasted or relationships that have failed. Do not let this dissuade you from your goal of recovery, It's important to remember that each time you face and confront another one of these obstacles, recovery is that much closer at hand.

How to Use This Workbook

Just as it is important to realize that the process of recovery takes time, it is also important to know that determination and persistence will be required. Try to visualize this journey as a long hike, at times uphill, slow and plodding and requiring great effort and at other times downhill, a more leisurely stroll requiring less exertion but continued attention to the trail and its pitfalls. Generally, it is ill-advised to hike alone and that same rule holds true here. Having someone to share this experience with, someone to point out hazards on the way, someone to encourage you when you tire, and someone to help you see how far you've traveled is always of benefit on any journey. And, just as you would never begin a trek without necessary supplies, so too, there are items you will need on this trip. Be sure to have them with you at all times.

Those of us who have backpacked the Timberline Trail that goes around the top of Mount Hood in Oregon know that you hike up to a ridge and then down the other side over and over again as you circle the mountain. On such a trek in late August, you tiredly trudge to the top of a ridge only to be rewarded by the breathtaking beauty of a mountain stream surrounded by fields of wild flowers. Strolling through the valley while feasting on the view, you find yourself re-energized, ready for the next uphill climb. A couple of hours later, feeling fatigued but pleased with your progress, you make it to another rise where before you is spread out a white sheet of snow that you must carefully cross and later a roaring river that you must shimmy across on a fallen tree trunk.

Recovery from LSE is a similar adventure following a labyrinth-like path of twists and turns, often uphill and often both tiring and demanding, yet with small victories along the way that outweigh the adversity and that stimulate you to continue moving forward. In this journey, you are encouraged to take time to smell the flowers as you go—to celebrate your progress. Don't rush—new skills and attitudes are built over time. But don't loiter either; progress is best made by continually plodding along the trail. So, determinedly keeping your eyes on the goal, continue to place one foot in front of the other, moving steadily onward. As you do, you will begin to envision a new future and renewed hope that you can fulfill your dreams.

Do what you can. Some people have jobs and schedules that will allow them to incorporate these exercises into their work life. Others do not so that the time they have available to focus on this journey must be relegated to early mornings, noon hours, evenings, and weekends. People who are often on the road or in the air as a part of their job can use these periods of commuting to routinely and frequently practice reshaping their thinking for long periods of time, while others will have to work it into already busy lifestyles. Just remember, your success and the timeliness in which you reach your destination is directly related to the amount of time you devote to the journey and the consistency with which you follow the instructions. As with anything worth achieving, dogged determination and effort are required.

So now you are ready to begin. Best wishes for a successful and rewarding journey of recovery! Others have attained freedom and a new life through this process. You can do it too!

You will need only the following things to begin this journey:

1.   Your own unused copy of this workbook

2.   A copy of ***Breaking the Chain of Low Self-Esteem.*** You will be required to read ***Breaking the Chain...*** as you work through this book.

3.   A supply of 3x5 cards and a notebook, or a ***Self-Esteem Recovery Toolkit*** Toolkits can be purchased at www.TheSelfEsteemInstitute.com or through bookstores nationwide.

How to use this Workbook

1.   There are two possible ways to use this workbook.

You may work straight through the workbook, doing Obstacle 1, then Obstacle 2 followed by Obstacle 3, then Obstacle 4, and then Obstacle 5. For those of you that need to feel the orderliness of doing it this way, feel free to do so. It is what most of us are used to and seems most logical. If you choose to do it this way you must read ***Breaking the Chain of Low Self-Esteem*** in it's entirety before beginning as this book is a companion to ***Breaking the Chain...***

Or you may follow the optional directions indicated by the following sign:

Throughout Obstacles 1, 2, 3, and 4, this "arrow" is placed to guide you in an alternate way of using this workbook, *which the author recommends.* The arrows direct you to read chapters from ***Breaking the Chain...* or to move to a different section of this book where you will work on a different Obstacle for a time.** Using the workbook this way will mean moving back and forth between sections so that you are eventually working on the whole of your self-esteem recovery at one time. This is the way recovery would be handled in therapy where you would work on more than one issue at a time. This method has proven to aid the LSE sufferer in seeing his progress in day to day challenges rather than feeling that he is merely gaining new information. Additionally, because you are working on all of the issues at the same time, your insight into one Obstacle will help you better understand the big picture of what recovery entails and what the final goal is. **Finally, this method may be the fastest form of recovery, if you do all that you are instructed to do.**

2. When you are directed to read a portion from the book, ***Breaking the Chain of Low Self-Esteem***, always do so. Even if you have already read the book in its entirety, refreshing your memory by rereading the segments suggested at the appropriate time will be very critical to your recovery progress.

3. Don't skip the explanations in each section. They contain new information not mentioned in the mother book. Similarly, don't skip over portions that seem tedious. Instead, if you need to, take a break and come back to the work at another time.

4. Devote time to this workbook on a regular basis. Whether daily or twice a week, try to *schedule regular periods of uninterrupted time* for these exercises. Allowing too much time to pass between sessions will slow or retard your progress, causing you to become discouraged.

5. If you are in therapy, ask your therapist to work with you. This additional motivation and accountability often proves helpful to most people.

6. When you finish with the workbook, your recovery work will not be complete. Instead, Obstacle 5, your last Obstacle will include instruction on the next phase of recovery where you will begin using a notebook and your Self-Esteem Recovery Cards (*or a Self-Esteem Recovery Toolkit*). Be sure to do so. It is strongly recommended that you use your **Self-Esteem Recovery Cards** on a regular basis, preferably 5 times a day. Just as a recovering alcoholic must continue to fight the urge to drink, you will need to continue the fight against the proclivity for negative thinking that you have practiced most of your life. Continue to use them until you have developed new thinking patterns and find that LSE is seldom a problem in your life. This is the ongoing work of overcoming LSE without which your recovery will be thwarted and your present progress will likely regress.

The journey of recovery from low self-esteem involves restructuring your life. If you persist to the end of this pilgrimage, you—and your life—will never be the same. Instead, you will gain control of your thinking and be able to make conscious choices that are no longer based on fear or anxiety. You will become more balanced and self-assured, no longer avoiding unfamiliar situations or trying to protect yourself from invisible threats. As you become more confident and less needy, you will make better decisions in relationships and learn who and when to trust. As you become more discerning and aware of your self-defeating behavior, you will be able to end the self-sabotage that has held you back.

All in all, you are about to embark on one of the most profoundly life-altering experiences possible, which will affect every aspect of your being. All that is required is that you keep your eyes on the possibility of an abundant and fulfilling life—a prospect that was snatched from you long before you could even imagine it. Those with LSE can recover from it to the point where they seldom face a problem related to low self-esteem; on the rare occasion when LSE then does flare up, they will find that the experience is neither debilitating nor long-lasting, but one they can control.

The path to recovery is difficult, wearing, and at times monotonous. And while there is no shortcut to overcoming low self-esteem, remember that this may be the most important journey you ever take—with an outcome that will affect the rest of your life.

Do not attempt to race madly to the finish line or even to complete the trek quickly; instead as hikers on a long journey, begin steadily plodding down the trail. Anticipate picking up speed with each new insight until one day without warning you realize that your pace seems quicker, your pack lighter, and your hope of recovery has increased. Just remember that such an expedition requires time, patience, determination, and persistence, so begin with hope and keep pressing on.

OBSTACLE 1

Introduction: Recognizing the Problem

People operate largely on the basis of the beliefs they hold about themselves and their own capabilities, convictions rooted in their experiences from birth. Those who believe they are capable are generally more motivated and able to express their creativity because they have confidence that they will succeed. On the other hand, those who have concluded that they are inadequate fear failure and are less inclined to place themselves in situations where this insufficiency might be apparent to themselves or others.

The most important step in the journey to overcome LSE, of course, is realizing you have low self-esteem. The fact that you are now beginning this workbook is a clear indication that you have already developed that awareness, so congratulations to you! Many people go through life never realizing that LSE is their real issue or never being able to fully acknowledge it. Hopefully you have not gone through many years of misdirected therapy and hopefully you also recognize that the symptoms of depression, fear and anxiety, anger, etc that have been inhibiting your ability to live a satisfying life are likely attributable to a damaged self-esteem, but a repairable one. If you are looking at this workbook, but are unsure if you have low self-esteem, it is recommended that you read the book, ***Breaking the Chain of Low Self-Esteem*** and that you also take the questionnaire at the end of chapter one in that book. These two activities should clarify whether or not you are one of the millions who suffer from this problem.

As you learn more about what it means to have low self-esteem, you will also begin to realize how serious a problem this is, that you are one of millions who regularly suffer from this condition. And, you will realize you have nothing to be ashamed of: you did not cause your low self-esteem. Because of you have struggled with LSE, you probably also realize that overcoming this problem will not be a quick fix, that you have an extensive journey ahead. Don't expect your attitudes or behaviors to change quickly. Instead the results may well be invisible at first; however, they will become more visible over time. At times you may feel discouraged and think that you aren't getting anywhere—this is to be expected, since negative thinking is what those with LSE do best. At other times, you will see glimpses of improvement and later still you will be able to see and feel your progress more clearly. Remember this when the work gets tedious and demanding: progress towards recovery will also be exciting and can be forever rewarding.

NOTE:

*Obstacle 2: The next section, **Rewriting the Script** focuses on becoming aware of, then altering the irrational and distorted thinking that begins with the development of low self-esteem and remains until recovery is accomplished.*

*Obstacle 3: **Establishing the Source of Your LSE** involves discovering the source of your low self-esteem, how it was formed in the first place, so that the original distortions can be unearthed, revealed for what they are, and eliminated. Since children are born unable to analyze or draw conclusions, it stands to reason that the negative tapes each LSE sufferer carries around were formed by input from the people and circumstances in his early life. Certainly his LSE did not begin as the result of an innate critical spirit or from being born thinking he was inferior, unlovable, or undeserving. Being able to pinpoint how one's self-esteem developed also provides a new perspective on the validity of the inner tape and its conclusions.*

*Obstacle 4: **Catching Up**, discusses how those with LSE fail to acquire specific and necessary basic life skills, articulates what those skills might be, and asks pointed questions that will help you assess your needs in each area.*

*Obstacle 5: **Completing the Journey**, fully explains what you will need to do after finishing this workbook. Completing the exercises will give you the tools to continue the recovery process on your own.*

➲   *Please read or reread **Chapter 1, "Low Self-Esteem: What is It?"** of **Breaking the Chain of Low Self-Esteem** (pages 9-27) before continuing. Answer the Questionnaire at the end of that chapter and then return to this page.*

UNDERSTAND: *The journey you are beginning is one that is not well known or well traveled. Even most psychologists, psychiatrists, and social workers don't believe that low self-esteem is a valid disorder; they have not been trained to see it as a serious problem that must be addressed directly. Instead, most professionals think that there are degrees of self-esteem and that LSE fluctuates, so that at one time a person has high self-esteem and on another day, week, or month, her self-esteem may be lower. Most therapists view low self-esteem as a symptom of other disorders in the same way a cough is a symptom* *of a cold or of bronchitis. Consequently, many of these professionals ignore or barely touch on self-esteem issues and treat the client's depression, stress, or anxiety, believing that the self-esteem problem will vanish when he gets over his depression, when he removes the stress in his life, when he overcomes his anxiety. Many recommend medication for these issues, when, in fact, medication is generally unnecessary and in most cases only masks the symptoms and does nothing to alter the underlying problems.*

In other words, these professionals don't understand that low self-esteem stands alone—it's not caused by other issues but can only be exacerbated by them. Such therapists may even use the words "low self-esteem," but they do not recognize the seriousness of it—that it is a pervasive pattern of thinking that never leaves a person, that it is a nagging self-doubt that always lingers below the surface, and that it is accompanied by a constant fear that controls people's lives.

*If you have already read the book, **Breaking the Chain of Low Self-Esteem**, you may well understand far better than most mental health professionals what low self-esteem is all about. And because awareness is the first step to resolving any problem, you're already on your way. If you are just beginning to read **Breaking the Chain...** you will be developing your awareness as you read on and you will be far ahead of most people in your knowledge of how LSE permeates every part of a person's life. You may even want to share this awareness with a professional someday, so that she can use her other many other skills to assist you in your recovery.*

Facts to Remember as you Begin

1. ***You need not be ashamed that you have LSE.***

    You may have been ridiculed for admitting you have LSE or for acting in ways that indicate you do. People may have told you to "just get over it," implying that you could alter the way you feel if only you tried. Others may have told you that you're just "too sensitive." This is not only discomforting, these are the kind of statements that have likely led to your self-esteem issues in the first place, fueling your self-doubts, invalidating your experiences, provoking you, and inciting your rage. The truth is that you can't "just get over it," for low self-esteem is a conditioned process of faulty thinking that must be corrected, a way of approaching life that must be analyzed and altered.

    If you have low self-esteem, you need not be ashamed, even though society unwittingly may suggest you should be, for you did not cause your low self-esteem and you are not responsible for having developed the view of yourself that you now hold. Because you now recognize that you have LSE, however, the ball is now in your court, and from this moment on you must assume full responsibility for what you do about it—whether you continue to let it destroy your life and cause you to self-sabotage your dreams, or whether you choose to put forth the considerable amount of effort, persistence, and determination necessary to free yourself from the chains that have kept you in bondage. Obviously, because you are beginning the trek through this workbook, you have decided to take charge and do what is necessary to reclaim your right to a full life.

2. ***LSE is a serious problem.***

    While you recognize that low self-esteem has negatively affected your life, it's also important to realize that LSE is a serious problem, not just for you, but in the world and across cultures. Everyone who experiences these feelings of doubt about their competence, adequacy, worthiness, or their ability to love and be found loveable, also experiences the profound and broad scope of the negatively devastating effects of this problem in their lives.

3. ***LSE is your core issue.***

    Don't let anyone dissuade you or convince you otherwise. Don't let those who call it merely a symptom of something else alter your course. Don't let friends or family persuade you that you are just selfish or that you could just change the way you feel if you wanted to bad enough. The depression, the anxiety and fear in social settings, the unexplained rages, or even the eating disorder that you may have struggled with are clear indications that you suffer from low self-esteem—simple to say, tough to understand and tougher still to alter. Even professionals who don't treat self-esteem as a core issue will tell you that low self-esteem is at least a symptom. But how can the basic way you view your life and yourself be only a symptom when in fact, depression, anxiety, anger, etc. are emotional reactions? What then are they reactions to, if not to the way the person sees herself and her ability to cope in the world. The exceptions to this rule, of course, are that of chronic illnesses due to other factors such as debilitating depression due to chemical unbalances in the body, totally unrelated mental issues such as psychosis, behaviors due to brain disorders or injuries, etc. Certainly, LSE is not the cause of every mental problem. It is, however, the most frequent cause of anxiety, depression, dependency, anger, eating disorders, and inability to handle social situations with ease.

    You may even read magazine articles or hear television commercials that suggest you have social anxiety disorder, because the symptoms of that disorder are actually the same features that you have experienced with low self-esteem. Again, with this disorder, however, LSE is viewed as only a symptom meaning that low self-esteem would not be the focus of treatment.

4. ***You may need to distance yourself from some of the people in your life while in recovery.***

During this time of recovery, your energy and your concentration will be taxed, and your emotions may feel very close to the surface and easily activated. Consequently, it is a good idea to remove yourself, to the extent possible, from those people in your life who provoke, intimidate, and discourage you, or who in any other way are less than supportive. Parents often fit into this category because quite often they are the ones who neglected you, criticized you, abused you, failed to protect you, abandoned you, or in some other way contributed to or caused the development of your low self-esteem in the first place. And they may well continue to be critical of who you are and what you do. If this is true for you and you live near your parents, you may want to decrease the frequency and length of visits or phone calls to them: You may want to make other plans for where you spend your holidays, or make additional plans so that you can leave after a short stay. This will serve to limit periods in uncomfortable situations where your low self-esteem may be further damaged. It will be even more difficult to work through your recovery issues if you allow those responsible for shaping your negative and distorted thinking in the first place to continue inundating you with the same destructive behaviors and attitudes. Therefore, it is your responsibility to protect yourself from environments and people who do not encourage healthy, respectful, and appropriate communication and actions.

Similarly, if friends, siblings, or coworkers discourage you, ridicule you, or undercut your efforts, look for ways to separate from them or limit contact.

Having an unsupportive spouse or partner will be more difficult, of course, and if you find yourself in that situation, other questions become apparent, such as "Why are you in this relationship?" and "How does your low self-esteem enter into such a relationship?" This is not a suggestion to leave the relationship, but merely a recommendation that as you go through this process, you consider your role in your primary relationship and ways in which you might alter the dynamics. In the meantime, however, you will need some outside affirmation to counterbalance your partner's lack of approval as you focus on recovery.

5. ***Support will greatly aid you in your recovery process.***

In this journey as well as in most aspects of our lives, having someone in our corner increases the likelihood that we will succeed. This means, of course, being willing to share what you are going through with another person, which can create feelings of vulnerability and fear. Because you suffer from low self-esteem, you may not have developed relationships in which you bared your soul for fear the other person would think you were inadequate. Or you may have established relationships with others who have low self-esteem because you thought similarly, never realizing that you both suffered from the same core issue.

If your LSE stems in part from never receiving the support you needed, even as a child, you may be especially fearful of opening up to another individual because your experience has taught you that others might use this information against you. Thus, developing a support group may be a part of your recovery work.

In the meantime, observe the people in your life, looking for someone who seems to genuinely care about you, someone who has proven to be trustworthy, someone with whom you feel comfortable. If you find one or more such individuals, share a little information about your issues and plans for recovery, limiting what you share to a small amount at a time to see how the person responds. If you continue to feel safe, respected, and affirmed by this person, you may have found the support person you need, the person with whom you can share your ups and downs, your progress, and what you are learning about yourself.

Some who suffer from low self-esteem find that they don't have anyone in their lives with whom to establish such a relationship. They may choose instead to enter therapy for guidance and support and to rely on their therapist for support until they gain the skills to find people with whom they can establish a healthy and mutually gratifying relationship. Whether you now have that significant advocate in your life, remember that finding one or more such friends is an important goal. Such a friend will not only help you in your recovery but can serve as a stable source of feedback when tough decisions arise or when you need to check out your perceptions.

6. **There is no quick fix. Recovery takes time.**

Try to be patient with your recovery process and the journey you must take to get there. Once LSE attitudes and beliefs are established and when they have been practiced for years, they stubbornly resist change. Be patient with yourself, be persistent, and remain determined. Recovery will come.

7. **Medication is seldom necessary for those with LSE.**

It is unlikely that you will need to use medication in order to recover from low self-esteem; however, because of the professional and cultural misunderstanding about what low self-esteem is, many therapists may recommend medicine as a solution. In most cases, pills are not a remedy but merely a means of masking the symptoms so that you will not feel the same intensity of fear or anxiety, but the drug will change none of the underlying patterns of behavior and self-doubt that led to these issues. If and when they go off the medication, their symptoms gradually return in full force. On rare occasions, some individuals who suffer from extremely low self-esteem may need to use medication as a temporary measure to even be able to begin the process of recovery. This might be the case for LSE sufferers whose social skills are seriously impaired due to years of isolation and whose anxiety levels are excessively high. For most LSE victims, however, medicine is not needed.

8. *Using the "Feelings List"*

Throughout the workbook you will be asked to choose words from the *Feelings List* that best describe how you feel or felt at a specific time in your life. This is a very extensive list and is intended to be so, to help you refine your understanding of exactly what you feel. We are all familiar with the experience of being asked, "How's it going?" or "How are you doing?" All too often the question is really a greeting rather than a question and we don't seriously consider the answer but respond, "Fine. How about you?" Additionally, most people have a habit of defining how they feel with the following twelve words or something close to them: fine, good, great, depressed, discouraged, sad, angry, frustrated, exhausted, stressed, concerned, and upset. Yet, you will see on the Feeling List that there are a great many more possibilities to choose from though you will likely have to think longer to be able to discern the differences and to choose the precise words for the situation.

➲   *Take a moment to preview the* **Feelings List** *on the next two pages and then move on to* **Obstacle 2***, page 19.*

Feelings List

Abandoned	Bewildered	Deficient	Exploited
Abnormal	Blamed	Defiled	Exposed
Abused	Blindsided	Defeated	Fearful
Accepted	Blue	Defenseless	Fooled
Accused	Bored	Degraded	Flustered
Accosted	Bothered	Dejected	Foolish
Adequate	Brave	Demeaned	Forgotten
Admonished	Browbeat	Dependent	Forlorn
Adrift	Bruised	Depressed	Fortunate
Afraid	Brutalized	Deserted	Frantic
Aggravated	Buttonholed	Deserving	Frazzled
Aggressive	Caged	Desperate	Frightened
Aghast	Calm	Despairing	Furious
Agitated	Capable	Despondent	Grateful
Alarmed	Castrated	Destroyed	Guarded
Alone	Cautious	Detached	Guilty
Aloof	Censored	Determined	Happy
Amazed	Challenged	Devalued	Harassed
Ambushed	Chaotic	Devastated	Hassled
Amused	Chastened	Disappointed	Hated
Angry	Cheap	Discarded	Hateful
Annoyed	Cheated	Discounted	Heartsick
Anxious	Cheerless	Discouraged	Heartbroken
Appalled	Chided	Disgraced	Helpless
Apologetic	Childish	Disgusted	Hopeful
Appreciated	Comforted	Disillusioned	Hopeless
Apprehensive	Comfortable	Disinterested	Horrified
Ashamed	Competent	Disloyal	Hostile
Assaulted	Concerned	Dismissed	Humble
Assertive	Condemned	Disrespected	Humiliated
Assured	Confined	Distressed	Hurt
Astonished	Conflicted	Disturbed	Idiotic
Attacked	Confused	Dominated	Indignant
Attractive	Contempt	Doublecrossed	Ignorant
Avenged	Content	Downcast	Ignored
Awkward	Contradicted	Dumfounded	Immature
Bad	Controlled	Edgy	Impatient
Baffled	Cornered	Embarrassed	Implicated
Battered	Courteous	Empty	Impotent
Beat-Up	Cowardly	Energized	Important
Befuddled	Crazy	Enraged	Incensed
Believed	Criticized	Entangled	Inadequate
Belittled	Crushed	Enthusiastic	Indifferent
Beloved	Dazed	Envious	Ineffective
Berated	Deceived	Exasperated	Inferior
Betrayed	Defamed	Exhausted	Ignored

Incapacitated	Neglected	Scarred	Uncared-for
Inconsolable	Nervous	Scolded	Unclean
Inconsequential	Numb	Scorned	Underestimated
Indebted	Obligated	Screwed	Undeserving
Indecent	Offended	Second-rate	Undesirable
Indecisive	Overcome	Selfish	Undercut
Indifferent	Overlooked	Sensitive	Underdeveloped
Injured	Overwhelmed	Sensual	Undermined
Inhibited	Pained	Sentimental	Uneasy
Innocent	Paralyzed	Shaky	Unimportant
Insecure	Passive	Shamed	Unlovable
Insignificant	Patronized	Shocked	Unloved
Isolated	Penalized	Short-changed	Unlucky
Insulted	Persecuted	Shutdown	Unprotected
Intense	Pessimistic	Shutout	Unsatisfied
Intimidated	Phony	Shy	Unloved
Intruded upon	Pissed	Sick	Unskilled
Invaded	Pitiful	Sickened	Unstable
Invalidated	Pleased	Sideswiped	Unwanted
Invisible	Powerless	Slapped	Unworthy
Involved	Proud	Sleazy	Upset
Irate	Provoked	Smothered	Up-Tight
Irrelevant	Pummeled	Speechless	Used
Irritated	Puzzled	Stabbed	Useless
Jealous	Quashed	Startled	Valuable
Joyous	Queasy	Stereotyped	Violated
Judged	Raped	Stressed	Vulgar
Justified	Rebellious	Stubborn	Vulnerable
Lacking	Rebuked	Stung	Wary
Lethargic	Rejected	Stunned	Wasted
Listless	Relieved	Stupid	Weak
Livid	Remorseful	Subdued	Weary
Lonely	Repressed	Submissive	Whipped
Lonesome	Reprimanded	Successful	Wicked
Lost	Reproached	Suicidal	Wild
Lovable	Repulsed	Sullen	Withdrawn
Loved	Resentful	Supported	Witty
Mad	Resigned	Susceptible	Wonderful
Maligned	Respected	Suspicious	Worn-out
Miserable	Responsible	Taunted	Worthless
Misled	Resentful	Tense	Worthy
Misrepresented	Restless	Terrified	Wounded
Misunderstood	Restrained	Threatened	Wronged
Mistaken	Restricted	Tormented	
Misused	Retarded	Trampled	
Mocked	Rewarded	Trapped	
Mortified	Ridiculed	Tricked	
Motivated	Robbed	Ugly	
Nauseated	Sad	Unappreciated	
Needy	Satisfied	Unattractive	

Obstacle 2

Rewriting the Script

As human beings, we have the ability to retain large quantities of information and feedback, our minds functioning much like a videotape, capable of both storing and retrieving information. When compiled, these serve as the basis for our belief system. Emblazoned on the videotape of our minds and reinforced through recurring memories of past events, we see and accept the basic beliefs of this script as the ultimate truth. We all have such a videotape, which lays the foundation for our motivation, dreams, and choices. This tape is cemented in our thoughts and is extremely difficult to alter. Thus, the first things we learn as children tend to be what we believe about ourselves and our world until or unless some form of dissonance causes us to seriously review them and come to a different conclusion.

What makes this tape so damaging? Unlike the script that holds the life story of a person with healthy self-esteem, the video of the person with low self-esteem contains primarily negative and disparaging feedback. In other words, it sets a pessimistic tone that seeps into every crevice of the mind, contaminating thoughts, eroding confidence, and blinding that individual to the truth. Furthermore, this tape is the main source of information from which a person draws his conclusions about himself, his worth, his competence, and his ability to meet life's challenges. Thus if the situations that he has encountered ended poorly, if the behaviors of others toward him were destructive, and if the feedback that he received early in life was primarily negative, his tape will be negative. His tape will be filled with painful events and negative experiences that say he is unworthy, inadequate, and unlovable; he will have developed low self-esteem. Without recovery from LSE, this tape will continue to be a daily reminder of his inadequacy.

Unfortunately, the person with low self-esteem doesn't realize that her tape is the product of inaccurate interpretations and the conduct of unhealthy or simply less-than-perfect people who, well intentioned or not, passed on their own shortcomings to the children under their watch. The young child cannot sort out the fact that the messages these adults have relayed, whether by word or deed, are full of distortions based on their own inadequacies; she cannot tell that these messages are, therefore, inaccurate and misleading. The child on the receiving end of this communication has no way of analyzing what is true and what is not. Beginning at birth, she had to rely on those older and in charge, naturally believing their negative words, naturally interpreting their inappropriate actions toward her as warranted. Just as naturally, she has acted accordingly. The end result is that she thinks of herself as less adequate than others, and becomes motivated by rage, paralyzed by fear, or falls somewhere in between these two extremes, prompting her to act in ways that are self-defeating. Consequently, she spends her life with negative, inhibiting, and hurtful misconceptions about herself—-misconceptions that contribute to every present or future choice and action—or failure to act.

In other words, our tape becomes our frame of reference, what we turn to when making decisions, what we use to interpret the degree of threat in the situations we encounter, and what we refer to when forming our beliefs about ourselves and the world.

Interestingly, this process of interpreting the behavior of others and then drawing conclusions all takes place in the individual's mind, in our thinking. Fellow LSE sufferers may instantly sense the threat or conflict being experienced by their comrades, but other non-sufferers will have no idea what the person with low self-esteem is saying to herself, nor will they be aware of how she is processing information. Unconscious of their own positive videotape, they will be oblivious of the negative one in the head of the person with low self-esteem as well as the negative content it contains. Instead, people with healthy self-esteem assume that others think as they do and are often surprised by the responses or fears of the person with low self-esteem, should she ever share it.

Conversely, while the person with low self-esteem starts out believing that all people think alike, he very quickly begins to see that others respond differently than he can or does. He recognizes that others are less often offended and seem better able to take in stride what goes on around them, and that others seem more capable of adjusting to new situations than he is. Naturally, because of his experience and the instant, spontaneous replaying of his negative tape, the person with low self-esteem interprets from this that he is abnormal. Whether consciously or unconsciously, he tells himself that he must be careful to avoid situations where his inadequacies will be visible and where the potential exists for others to exhibit disapproval or to reject him.

Each of us talks to ourselves all day, every day; in fact, its been said we each make between 20,000 and 40,000 self-statements each day. At issue here is *what* we tell ourselves, *because the content of our self-talk is what controls our lives.* For those with LSE, self-talk is the ball and chain that keeps them imprisoned and in misery.

Tony: Distorted self-talk

As a child, Tony developed low self-esteem and the negative self-talk that always accompanies it. Now a junior in high school, when a teacher asks him a question in class, he tells himself, "She doesn't like me and is picking on me." He even reasons that the teacher knows he won't have the answer and is mocking him. When he can't answer the question, Tony silently berates himself for being so dumb. When a girl sincerely smiles at him, Tony tells himself, "She's just laughing at me and trying to embarrass me by acting like she likes me." When he considers befriending or dating someone, Tony decides that it's too risky and that it would be too embarrassing to ask because she surely won't want to date him. When his mother asks him how his day went, Tony responds rudely, telling himself that "she isn't really interested in my day. She's just checking up on me." When the boss at his last part-time job pointed out an error he had made, Tony concluded that the man didn't like him; now, when a similar incident occurs at his new job, Tony inaccurately jumps to the conclusion that he is about to be fired, prompting him to consider quitting before this happens.

In each incident, Tony misreads the behavior and intentions of others, concluding that all see him as inferior or inadequate in some way. Each time Tony makes such an inaccurate judgement, he is acting in a self-defeating manner wherein his self-statements interfere with his goals. His first thought always has a negative slant in that he surmises that the other person is thinking disapprovingly about him. In each case, this negative self-talk leads to poor results: feeling bad because he perceives others are laughing at him, not attempting to befriend girls whom he finds attractive and interesting, denying himself a close relationship with his mother, and unnecessarily quitting a job. This is typical behavior for those with low self-esteem: the more severe the low self-esteem, the more prevalent these negative thoughts and actions.

Altering this self-talk, the second Obstacle that must be faced, must be the primary focus for overcoming low self-esteem.

> **REMEMBER:** *Getting beyond Obstacle 2 is not simple nor can it be accomplished quickly, for when we have practiced a way of thinking all of our life, it is a formidable challenge to face the fact that many of the constructs upon which we have based our lives are untrue. Instead, much like the challenge of making your way through an obstacle course full of holes and ruts, with fallen trees to scale, creek beds to wade through, and hills to climb, the journey is difficult, uncomfortable, tiring, and redundant. Altering our way of talking to ourselves requires that we learn to recognize, edit, and replace the destructive process of inaccurate and irrational talk. First we must become aware of how this negative—and*
>
> *cont.*

inaccurate self-talk is a means of self-sabotage and a way of protecting ourselves at a very high cost. Second, we must become aware **of how often we talk to ourselves this way, how frequently our messages are distorted, and what these specific messages are.**

⮕   *Before continuing, please read* **Chapter 2, "Facing Fear and Anxiety," of Breaking the Chain of Low Self-Esteem** *(pages 33-67).*

A Journey into Patterns of Low Self-Esteem Thinking

Developing new patterns first requires awareness of the present ones. The following pages and examples will help you become more conscious of how people with low self-esteem think. Many of us think that we are the only one who thinks like this or acts in self-defeating ways, but these examples will demonstrate patterns that are common to *all* people who suffer from low self-esteem. The frequency and depth of a person's response depends on the seriousness of his low self-esteem, which varies from individual to individual, *and* on the extent to which he perceives a situation as threatening. Thus, all LSE sufferers are to some extent anxious and fearful, and they routinely say negative things to themselves about themselves, escalating their anxiety to even more extreme levels in situations where people with healthy self-esteem would experience minimal or no discomfort. Thus, the LSE sufferer comes into every situation with some anxiety based on years of self-doubt. When a new and thus unfamiliar opportunity arises, he tries to analyze it, looking for similarities to past negative events. If he finds any such similarities, he inevitably concludes that the threat of rejection is too great, that the possibility of saying or doing something inappropriate is too risky. Fearful of making a mistake and embarrassing himself, he finds a reason to avoid the event.

People with severe low self-esteem have developed LSE as the result of an exceptionally dysfunctional background, whether as the result of neglect or abandonment, consistently harsh criticism and disapproval, or abuse. Many feel emotionally disabled, fully aware that they don't know what is appropriate behavior in most new situations. They may be equally aware that they don't have the skills to cope that others seem to possess. Even more confusing, they don't know how much they don't know or when what they think they know is inaccurate, causing them to feel very vulnerable. Such LSE sufferers are more likely to experience fear and anxiety in nearly all situations they encounter, while others with mild to moderate LSE may only experience this trepidation in specific areas of their lives, often in the social arena where there is no "cookbook" on what to do, on what to say, or on how to interpret the behavior or expectations of others.

After it surfaces, the fear, anxiety, and discomfort may propel the person with LSE to respond in ways he will regret and later castigate himself for. Or he will fail to respond in ways he later realizes he should have, causing more reason for alarm when faced with the next unfamiliar situation. Experiencing several of these excruciating events can be sufficiently painful to convince him to quit trying, to avoid future involvement, and to isolate. Some LSE sufferers will become enraged with both themselves and their environment and, on occasion, they will act out their hostile feelings.

REMEMBER: *Everyone—with or without LSE—experiences fear and anxiety. This is not unusual and we will never be able to entirely rid ourselves of either one. The difference, however, is that LSE sufferers become fearful and anxious in situations where no obvious danger is present and where those with healthy self-esteem would experience little or no fear and anxiety. Thus, the experiencing of these emotions is irrational at these times because the fear and anxiety is not based on reality, not on a true and present danger, not on fact. Examples of situations in which those with LSE may experience this fear and anxiety are listed below. Notice that both the anticipation or consideration of an activity and /or the actual performance are anxiety-provoking and can thus be triggering events for a self-esteem attack. This is only a partial list; many more such situations exist.*

- anticipating attending a party; actually doing so
- thinking of asking someone out on a date; actually doing so
- considering taking college classes, signing up for the class, attending the class
- deciding whether or not to ask for a raise or promotion; actually doing so
- wanting to send food back in a restaurant because it isn't done right, tastes bad, or is not warm; actually doing so
- considering confronting someone about something they did or said; actually doing so
- returning an item that you purchased to the store; actually doing so
- sharing your opinion with a group of people that you don't know well
- sharing a differing opinion with anyone
- considering asking a new acquaintance to do something with you socially; actually doing so
- considering applying for a new job; actually doing so
- considering doing any new activity where you might look silly or inadequate; actually do so
- joining any type of new group where you don't know anyone

As you read this list, did other situations come to mind? Did you remember other examples that you have experienced? If so, list them below:

_____

_____

_____

_____

_____

_____

REMINDER:

- *It is strongly recommended that you do all of the exercises and that you do them in the order they are presented.*

- *Do not be concerned if you don't identify with each example given. Each person has experienced different situations, and those mentioned here are only intended to demonstrate a wide variety of possible scenarios and reactions in hope that you will identify with some and learn from the others.*

- *Additionally, do not be concerned if you don't have a lot of memories at first. When asked a question or when given instructions to describe a memory, do not fret if you seem to have none. People with LSE commonly have difficulty remembering, especially when all or parts of the memory are painful or when the person has practiced blocking out their recall of traumatic events.*

- *When trying to remember your past, focus on where you lived at that particular time, who the significant people were in your life, what grade you were in, what subjects you liked or disliked, what interests you had. Try to picture the rooms in your house, your bedroom. Try to remember your toys, your pets. Focusing on the surroundings can sometimes stimulate memories. Most importantly, don't get anxious because you can't remember—the memories will begin to come back the more you focus on the past.*

- *Try to answer the questions in order, but if you cannot remember any specifics to write down, go ahead and read through the section, stopping to pause when asked to write. If no memories come after three or four minutes, just continue this process until you come to the next section that tells you to read from **Breaking the Chain**... or to go work on a different obstacle. You can always come back to this as a later time.*

REMEMBER TOO: *The degree of fear and anxiety that any LSE sufferer experiences depends on the following factors:*

- *The level or seriousness of her low self-esteem and the subsequent degree of self-doubt she has about her abilities in that particular situation.* Thus, a person with *moderate* LSE will likely suffer more anxiety than an individual with *mild* LSE, and the person with *severe* LSE will suffer more anxiety than one with *moderate* LSE.

- *The specific circumstances surrounding the person's early environment and development.* For instance, someone knowledgeable about sports may not be as anxious about attending a football party as he would be about attending an office party where the conversation will likely be broader in content and might enter into realms in which he feels less adequate. Or someone who feels confident at his job may do fine at a work or at a business meeting where he is certain he knows the facts, but will experience extreme anxiety at a business luncheon, where more social skills are called for.

- *The significance the LSE sufferer places on the particular people involved or the outcome.* The LSE sufferer may feel totally comfortable around friends but experience extreme anxiety around coworkers whose opinions about her could affect how she is treated at work. Or an individual may feel extremely anxious and fearful about giving a presentation where his future father-in-law or someone else of significance will be present, knowing this person has the power to positively or negatively influence his future.

Thus, even among those with similar degrees of low self-esteem, the amount of anxiety each person experiences may vary. No one other than the LSE sufferer can realize the degree of foreboding or measure the impact experienced when anticipating or doing something he lacks confidence doing.

The twofold job of recovery from LSE, then, is to:

1. *Dismantle the dysfunctional puzzle, analyzing the pieces that created this problem called low self-esteem—the critical and damaging messages received in childhood and where they came from, and to dismantle the distorted and irrational thinking, the negative and inaccurate feedback that sufferers deliver to themselves, and the behavior that results.*

2. *Gradually begin altering the thinking patterns that accompany LSE so that we are free to make healthy choices and to behave in healthy ways.*

You will now embark on a pilgrimage toward recovery by taking a number of excursions that illuminate the experiences that those with low self-esteem encounter and the ways in which they react. In the same way that all education gives us a greater perspective, viewing the behavior of others not only broadens our understanding but can help us be more objective because our own emotions aren't involved. Additionally, examining the difficulties that others with LSE have faced can help us to realize that we are not alone—that the patterns of self-defeating behavior we exhibit are not uniquely strange but are rather typical of those who suffer from LSE. As you proceed on your journey you will move from observing the self-defeating thinking and behaviors of others to focusing on your own, which is essential for recovery.

   *Before continuing, please read **Chapters 3 and 4, "When Life is a Minefield"** and **"Ending the Self-Sabotage"** of **Breaking the Chain of Low Self-Esteem** (pages 75-123).*

After reading these chapters, return to page 27 in this workbook to continue your journey toward recovery.

Obstacle 2, Excursion A

How LSE Sufferers Program Themselves for Failure

Feelings are the result of thinking! Remember this premise. It's one of the most important ideas you will ever hear and one that will reshape your life if you believe it, remind yourself of it, and work with it. What does the phrase mean? Simply that you feel what you feel because of what you have just said to yourself, whether it's actually true or not. You perceive something, you talk to yourself about your observations or conclusions, and then feelings occur that are in line with your self-talk. These steps take place very quickly, almost instantaneously.

This isn't a problem if what you tell yourself is, in general, the truth. However, what LSE sufferers tell themselves is often distorted, inaccurate, and not based on fact; their self-statements are the conclusions of a frightened, lonely, underdeveloped, or under-socialized person. What if what you tell yourself is the result of information, values, and feedback taught you as a child by adults who were dysfunctional and unhealthy? What then will be the consequences for your life? A life controlled by LSE, a life filled with frustration, misery, anger, and remorse.

In Chapter 3 of **Breaking the Chain...** Paris talks himself out of going golfing with his coworkers after worrying that he may not be nearly as good as they are and may even make a fool of himself, how his coworkers would probably have negative thoughts about him and even talk about him among themselves, and how he would be anxious from then on wondering what they were thinking and saying about him. In other words, Paris talked to himself until he became so frightened and fearful that he had to refuse the invitation. This is typical behavior for those with moderate to severe low self-esteem.

As you embark on your journey, you will want to focus on the specific ways that you, like Paris, sabotage your own life by saying negative things to yourself which stir up negative emotions that prevent you from doing things you would like to do.

How thinking and self-talk dictate our feelings

2A-1. If we tell ourselves that we can't do something, we may be too *fearful* to try or we may sabotage our efforts if we do try. Thus if we are contemplating going back to college, we will tell ourselves that we are likely to fail and we may either decide not to enroll or find another way to self-destruct. We may go late to class, sit in the back, be too anxious to concentrate, block out what we know during tests, or not study enough *because we've already convinced ourselves it won't be productive.*

Did reading the above paragraph remind you of a time when you were too fearful to do something you really wanted to do? Describe your own example here.

Did go back to school. Have put off asking for letters of recommendation. Have often avoided going to social events d/t fear of failure/ridicule.

2A-2. If we tell ourselves that we are undeserving, we are less likely to ask for a raise, apply for a new position, or look for a better job. Maintaining the job we have will become more important than risking possible rejection. Can you think of a time when you have played it safe rather than risk possible rejection and later regretted it, wishing you had tried, or is there a time when you wondered what the outcome might have been if you'd taken that step? Describe that here.

Didn't go to Mexico to learn Spanish because I would have gone alone.

2A-3. If we tell ourselves that we aren't worthy of someone's attention, interest, or affection, we may feel inadequate and vulnerable, leading us to believe that approaching that individual would create too great a risk for rejection and disapproval. Or we might approach that person feeling self-conscious, awkward, and fearful, thereby not presenting ourselves well and setting ourselves up to fail. Describe something similar that has happened to you.

Have avoided going on dates, meeting new people d/t extreme fear of ridicule/rejection. I constantly do new situations in clinical, my fearfulness & awkwardness are obvious & don't present well.

_____

_____

_____

2A-4. If we tell ourselves that our opinions aren't valuable and that others don't want to hear them, we may not share our thoughts, instead remaining quiet and invisible. In doing so, we may go unnoticed and new acquaintances may not even remember us because we didn't share enough of ourselves or our ideas to make a memorable impression. Describe a time when this happened to you.

Current rotation: haven't & don't say what's on my
mind dt fear of conflict or retaliation. As result
most don't know me. Then when something
(?) was said about me, there was nothing to
counter it with.

_____

2A-5. If we tell ourselves others don't like us, we may avoid contact with people. If we tell ourselves we don't fit in at parties, we probably won't attend; if we do, we will be so anxious that we won't be able to be spontaneous and comfortable with ourselves or others. Do you sometimes feel that others don't like you? Does this keep you from attending functions or from being comfortable when you do? Write what you remember about such an occasion.

Have usually avoided parties or social events for
this reason. Example is upcoming student
party. Dread going.

_____

_____

_____

2A-6. If we are unwilling to look at our shortcomings or to examine the stages of development our dysfunctional families failed to teach us, we may not look for ways to grow or change, or even recognize the need to do so. Instead, telling ourselves we are okay the way we are, we will remain stagnant and continue to fall even further behind in our social development. The older we get, the more apparent this gap will appear and the harder to surpass. Do you ever feel that you are behind your peers in social development? In what social situations do you have the most difficulty?

Yes. New situations - especially when I have something @ stake. Most trouble c̄ groups - where I'm expected to be friendly.

2A-7. If we tell ourselves that we can't trust our decision-making, we may become— and remain—very dependent, looking for others to give us the answers and to direct our lives. This may lead us into relationships with unhealthy people who dominate and even abuse us. When have you gotten into a relationship because you were needy and wanted someone to give you the answers and tell you what to do so you didn't have to risk making a mistake? Describe this situation.

Todd - deferred excessively to his judgment & lately have found it not accurate. I should have gone to a neutral or prof'l person.

2A-8. If we downplay our talents by telling ourselves that we have nothing unique to offer, we may not pursue our creativity. Feeling too vulnerable to let others see our gifts for fear they will denigrate our work, we may not write those stories that are within us, paint those pictures we could so artfully produce, or invent those solutions that might enhance the lives of others. When have you found yourself fearful of exposing your creativity to others? When have you feared ridicule or criticism and either kept your talent hidden or ceased to use it? Give an example or two.

I am not aware of what my creativity is or of a talent I have.

_____

_____

_____

2A-9. If we tell ourselves we are less capable or less deserving than others, we may feel apathetic and unmotivated to create a better life for ourselves and set our aim in life too low. Believing that this is the best we can do, that we are fortunate to even be where we are now, or that we must settle for what we have, we may be incapable of seeking a better future, of dreaming of more than we now have, and we may not be inspired to set goals that would change our lives for the better. When have you given up your dreams and settled for less than you wanted? In what ways have you done this? Describe how and when you did this.

I have rejected potential partners d/t extreme fear of
it being revealed that I can't hold up my end. Am in a
dead-end situation where I'm not satisfied but am
afraid I can't have what I want.

_____

_____

2A-10. If we tell ourselves we are less important than others, we may feel hopeless about life, lowering our expectations of how others should treat us and of what we can expect from them. We may become passive, believing we don't have the right to assert ourselves or to confront those who mistreat us. When have you viewed yourself as less significant than others? In what ways did you expect either too much or too little of others?

Many ways

_____

_____

_____

_____

_____

2A-11. If we have difficulty trusting others and we become too watchful of those we love, we may constantly evaluate and scrutinize what they do to see if they really

love us. We may tell ourselves that they would act in specific ways if they truly
cared about us and we may misread their intentions or their behavior and feel
betrayed. Unless we communicate our fears and clarify our observations, we may
become alienated from those who care most about us. Do you have difficulty trusting
those who say they love you? What do they do or not do that causes you to suspect
they are not trustworthy?

My brother is only one who consistently says this.
Unfortunately, I am viewed as a child.

2A-12. If we tell ourselves that being a part of the world is too risky for us, we may isolate, experience extreme loneliness, and miss out on the many joys of life. When do
you find yourself intentionally isolating yourself out of fear? What types of situations might cause you to do so?

Often, Talk myself out of going to most social
situations.

2A-13. If once we've been successful, we continually tell ourselves that we're incapable
of maintaining that success, we may, in fact, spend our energy proving these negative self-statements. We may become too conservative and change the behaviors
that made us successful or in other ways sabotage ourselves. When have you sabotaged yourself after achieving success? How did you do this?

Got more fearful in last semester -
as graduation became nearer.

_____

_____

2A-14. If we fail to communicate our needs and desires because we tell ourselves we would feel too vulnerable or that we might be let down, we may feel dissatisfied and alone, failing to experience intimacy. Do you routinely fail to say what you want or need? Do you instead tend to defer to the wants and needs of others? Give examples.

Yes but will then defer my wants/needs to others if they're not met.

_____

_____

_____

_____

2A-15. If we constantly tell ourselves that others are out to get us or take advantage of us, we may feel on guard and angry, react defensively, and thwart the possibility of building new relationships. Do you find yourself angry much of the time? Do you feel others are out to get you? Give some examples.

Often resentful. Don't particularly feel others are out to get me. DO feel sometimes

_____

_____

_____

_____

2A-16. If we spend our time reminiscing about past hurts and feeding our anger and disappointment, we may become bitter people who regularly *"personalize" the behavior* of others and who are always on the defensive. For instance, we may jump to the conclusion that someone hasn't called because they don't like us, or we may think that our partner stays at work so late because he doesn't really want to come home. Personalizing means we interpret the behavior of others as always having something to do with us or as a reaction to us; we don't consider the many other reasons that others may have for doing what they do or don't do. When we con stantly personalize the actions of others, we may find people avoiding contact or involvement with us. Do you find yourself frequently hurt and your expectations unmet? Do you find yourself continually annoyed with others? Do you frequently think that people are trying to hurt you or shun you? Do you think you've lost friends or that relationships have suffered as a result of this critical evaluation of others? Explain.

Yes. Take too personally peoples actions or lack of

All these experiences demonstrate how *our thinking dictates our feelings*. These feelings then control our *behavior and our future thinking*. All are typical examples of those who have low self-esteem. This is how people with LSE *think about* themselves and *talk to* themselves *about* themselves. All of these patterns are dysfunctional and the result of a negative internal video. In contrast, people who have healthy self-esteem seldom program themselves in ways that are self-defeating. This is not to say that they succeed at everything they attempt, that they never do things they later regret, that they always know whom and when to trust, or that their relationships are always fulfilling. However, when those with healthy self-esteem talk to themselves, it is usually based on factual information; in general, they only give themselves negative feedback when it has proven true and then usually only about specific behaviors or a specific incident. For the most part, they do not over-generalize and exaggerate their faults the way those with low self-esteem do, nor are they self-condemning.

As you move on through the workbook, try to keep in mind that your feelings are caused by your thinking and not the other way around. Thus, when you feel badly these feelings are a signal to ask yourself what you have been thinking. This process of questioning your thinking is an all-important step in recovery and one you can begin now, even though your are just at the beginning of the journey.

    *Please go forward to **Obstacle 3, "Establishing the Source of Your LSE"** (page 105 in this book) and work through page 113. Instructions on page 113 will tell you where to go next.*

Intro to: Excursions B, C, D, E

Analyzing the Self-Defeating Process of Others

Your goal at this point is to begin developing an awareness of how people with low self-esteem talk to themselves in ways that are irrational and distorted and then perform behaviors that are self-defeating. As you travel along this path, you will begin to see what LSE sufferers think and say to themselves and how their *feelings are the result of this self-talk*. This concept bears repeating because, ultimately, these inaccurate self-statements are what control the lives of those with LSE. Understanding this is at the crux of beginning the process of recovery, for while our feelings cannot be altered simply by making a decision not to feel a certain way, *feelings can be transformed if the thoughts that precede them are altered.* Learning how to bring about that transformation is the ultimate aim of this journey of recovery.

REMINDER: As you work on the exercises, don't worry about what you write or how elegant it sounds. This is not a test. No one is evaluating your decisions or what you write. No one is grading your work. This exercise and the ones that follow are merely meant to increase your awareness of how LSE manages to affect and even control people's lives. You are not expected to be perfect now or ever.

Obstacle 2, Excursion B

The Difficulties of Starting a New Adventure

On Brittany's first day at her new job as director of advertising for a large soft-drink company, she is asked to attend a meeting and be introduced to the other employees. Brittany comes highly touted for her abilities and she is extremely talented; however, she has a problem. Contrary to what her excellent credentials might imply, Brittany has low self-esteem. As a result, she doesn't feel comfortable around new people, especially in large groups, or in unfamiliar situations where she doesn't know beforehand what will be expected of her. While Brittany knows she is efficient, creative, frequently complimented and rewarded, and highly respected, she nevertheless sees herself in a different light: she sees herself as socially inept, unattractive, and basically a misfit in spite of her abilities. She doesn't like to be the center of attention and she had hoped to meet her new colleagues just in the course of her work; certainly, she did not anticipate being formally introduced in front of the entire staff. From the moment she hears that she is expected to attend this big meeting, Brittany begins her pattern of negative self-talk, reminding herself of how awkward she is in large groups, telling herself that she should have worn a different outfit with a longer skirt, berating herself for not getting a haircut over the weekend. As she does so, her anxiety builds until she is shaking and nauseated.

Precisely five minutes before the meeting is to begin, Brittany forces herself to leave her office, careful to wait until others who are heading toward the conference room have passed by. Uptight but trying her best to look pleasant, Brittany enters the room, avoiding eye contact with anyone. Skilled at scoping out the least vulnerable or obvious place to sit, she quickly spots a row of empty seats and moves toward her selected "safe place" in the second to last row and on the aisle, providing an easy escape route, if necessary. Here, she thinks, others won't notice her or be able to watch her, and few will pass by as they enter the room. Gradually the staff file in, chatting and laughing, people who Brittany thinks obviously have a history together at this firm and maybe outside of work as well. Those who notice Brittany smile and nod a greeting; several men file into her row, say, "Hello" as they sit down, and then continue their conversations. A few minutes pass—awkward moments for Brittany, who purposely feigns examining her fingernails so she can keep her eyes lowered. No one would ever imagine at first glance that this unpretentious and seemingly shy woman could be the powerhouse her credentials describe.

The president calls the meeting to order and begins to introduce Brittany, "We expect Brittany's expertise, experience, and leadership to rekindle our company's marketing success. Brittany, would you please stand up so everyone can see you?" Inwardly, Brittany cringes but she rises to her feet and, with a smile pasted on her face, moves her eyes across the group of people who are now looking in her direction and clapping. Brittany, however, only sees eyes staring at her; she barely hears the sound of their clapping. She knows her face is now bright red, which embarrasses her more. Feeling her heart racing, she wishes she could vanish as she slides back into her seat.

The meeting continues and the focus shifts from her. But Brittany hears hardly anything. As soon as the meeting is over, she begins to make her way toward the door, forcing herself to stop only as long as she thinks she must, to shake hands and endure the welcoming chatter of those who approach her. Embarrassed that she blushed so when she was introduced, Brittany wants only to escape but knows that she must try to act polite and friendly.

2B-1. Looking at the scenario above, underline the ideas or events that might create anxiety or fear in a person with low self-esteem or that depict behavior associated with LSE and not with healthy self-esteem. For example, the phrase "On Brittany's first day at her new job" is one that would likely create at least minimal anxiety for anyone, but especially for a person with low self-esteem, since most people with LSE are unsure of themselves in new situations. The words "be introduced to the other employees" suggests a situation in which a person with low self-esteem will feel out of place, self-conscious, and vulnerable because she is surrounded by strangers.

Closely examining each sentence, underline any other words or phrases that represent things you think could create anxiety in Brittany before the meeting. Just relax and focus on Brittany and her story. Eventually, these exercises will involve your own scenarios. Underline the words or phrases before proceeding.

- Circle the phrases that you think would affect those with healthy self-esteem.
- How many phrases did you underline? _____
- Of the ideas you underlined, how many do you think would adversely affect individuals with healthy self-esteem? _____

2B-2. From your own experience, imagine what Brittany with her low self-esteem was saying to herself at each part of the day. For example, when receiving the invitation to the meeting, she might well have said to herself, "Oh, no. This is terrible. I hate big group meetings. I never know how to act or what to say. They will all be looking at me and will know how uncomfortable I am. I always do something stupid in groups. It will be awful."

Now you try it. Put yourself in Brittany's shoes. What might you be thinking if you were Brittany and you doubted your ability to do what was appropriate in new situations? What would you be saying to yourself if this were you? Would you be saying any positive things to yourself? Write those down as well. If you have difficulty with this exercise, don't worry. Over time and with practice, you will be able to predict with accuracy how others would respond in these situations. Most people are not aware of what they say to themselves, and those with low self-esteem may have an even more difficult time recalling their self-statements because they are so painful. Remember, this is just the beginning of the work, the beginning of your journey. If you were already proficient at these tasks, you wouldn't need this workbook.

Write down what you think Brittany might have been saying to herself:

- As she anticipates her first day at the new job:

_____

_____

_____

_____

- After arriving at work as she anticipates the upcoming meeting:

_____

_____

_____

_____

- As she waits for everyone to pass her office door before entering the hallway:

_____

_____

_____

_____

- As she enters the meeting room and looks for a seat in the back:

_____

_____

_____

_____

- As she examines her fingernails before the meeting begins:

_____

_____

_____

_____

- As the president introduces her and praises her:

_____

_____

_____

_____

- As she stands up while everyone looks at her:

_____

_____

_____

_____

- As she sits down, realizing her face is bright red and her heart is racing:

_____

_____

_____

_____

- As she tries to make her way toward the door on her way out:

  _____

  _____

  _____

  _____

- When the meeting is over and she sits alone in her new office:

  _____

  _____

  _____

  _____

This is a scenario that takes place in thousands of conference rooms every day. Some people in Brittany's position would waltz in, be introduced, soak up the applause and adulation, and schmooze with their new coworkers. Many, however, like Brittany are high achievers, often even overachievers, who excel at their work and nevertheless feel inadequate, especially in relating to other people. Like Brittany, they try to look normal and act normal all the while wondering what "normal" really is.

2B-3. Looking at the thoughts—the self-statements—that you listed in 2B-2,
- How many did you list? _____
- How many were negative? _____
- How many were positive? _____

Notice that people with low self-esteem primarily say negative things about themselves to themselves, increasing their anxiety and making it more likely that their performance may suffer and making it more likely that their fears will become self-fulfilling. Conversely, people with healthy self-esteem primarily say positive things to themselves, greatly increasing the likelihood that they will feel and look confident, capable, approachable, well rounded, and well adjusted. When they do give themselves negative feedback, it is usually specific and behavioral, with the focus immediately shifting to problem-solving or correcting the error. In contrast, the self-statements of those with LSE tend to be nonspecific, personally condemning, and irrationally generalized to their whole being rather than to a specific behavior. LSE sufferers frequently fall into the rut of obsessively focusing on the negative behavior or nagging self-doubts rather than using these thoughts as a springboard to constructive problem-solving and personal growth.

2B-4. Using the Feelings List (pages 16-17), select the words that best describe what you think Brittany was *feeling* after making the negative self-statements. For example, while she was looking at her fingernails, do you think she might have been feeling exposed? embarrassed? cornered? stupid? out-of place? Feel free to use words or phrases that are not on the list.

- As she anticipates her first day at the new job:

_____

_____

- As she anticipates the upcoming meeting:

_____

_____

- As she waits for everyone to pass her office door before entering the hallway:

_____

_____

- As she enters the meeting room and looks for a seat in the back:

_____

_____

- As she examines her fingernails before the meeting begins:

_____

_____

- As the president introduces her and praises her:

_____

_____

• As she stands up while everyone looks at her:

_____

_____

• As she sits down, realizing her face is bright red and her heart is racing:

_____

_____

• As she tries to make her way toward the door on her way out:

_____

_____

• When the meeting is over and she sits alone in her new office:

_____

_____

2B-5. Let's now imagine a different Brittany in the scenario above. Let's picture a Brittany with healthy self-esteem, a woman who likes herself, who enjoys the attention her success has brought her, who believes she is as competent as others in most ways and even more competent in some. This Brittany is someone who feels comfortable in social settings, who can engage with strangers, who accepts her appearance and who doesn't obsess about it, who feels deserving of what she has achieved.

With this in mind, rewrite the scenario, omitting or altering the words or phrases that you think would be different while leaving the basic story intact. Let your imagination flow. Take your time. There is no rush. If you have difficulty thinking how a person with healthy self-esteem would react, focus on simply removing the negative statements and writing the story without them. Each of these activities, whether meaningful to you now or not, will eventually come together to clarify LSE and the solution to it. The new scenario has been started for you, just complete the story.

On Brittany's first day at her new job as department head of advertising for a large soft-drink company, she is asked to attend a meeting and be introduced to the other employees.

Brittany comes highly touted for her abilities, is extremely talented, and is very confident about her new role.

In comparing Brittany's story to the one you have written, can you see that people with healthy self-esteem do not program themselves for negative outcomes in the way that LSE sufferers do? Can you see how those with healthy self-esteem and those with low self-esteem talk differently to themselves and that the negative self-statements of people with low self-esteem create an atmosphere and expectation of failure that produces anxiety and fear? Can you see that Brittany has a pattern of berating herself, and that her critical self-statements and negative thoughts set the stage for her negative emotions?

As we move through these early exercises, which involve situations other LSE sufferers have faced, it is important to realize that much like brainwashing, we can talk ourselves into or out of most anything. In other words, any one thought that we tell ourselves often enough will eventually become so ingrained in our minds that we will thereafter view it as fact or as the truth.

Secondly, once we have cemented that particular belief in our mind, it is extremely difficult to change. For instance, imagine after having been taught in your early education that 1+1=2, that someone now tells you that what you learned was wrong and that, in fact, 1+1=3. Would you be able to even entertain the possibility that you had been wrong all these years? We can quickly say, "Of course not," because we think that would be ridiculous. Consider, then, that it is not that much different for the person with low self-esteem, who sees herself as lacking in some way, based on beliefs that were formed in childhood, beliefs that she believes as strongly as the equation above. To change her perspective of herself is similarly difficult to even consider, let alone to actually accomplish. Thus, the work of recovery from low self-esteem is a difficult and complex one and it will take time, so be patient on this journey. Each exercise has a specific purpose and will gradually lead you from viewing these difficulties in others to being able to assess your own behavior and ultimately alter it.

Much as you did with Brittany's negative scenario, you will soon be able to concentrate on the scenario in Excursion C of Charles and how he copes with his low self-esteem, but first,

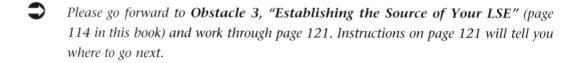

*Please go forward to **Obstacle 3, "Establishing the Source of Your LSE"** (page 114 in this book) and work through page 121. Instructions on page 121 will tell you where to go next.*

Obstacle 2, Excursion C

Awkward Social Situations

On the first Saturday of his college experience, Charles joins a group of guys, most of whom he doesn't know, in the dorm lounge to watch a football game. Though he pleaded that he didn't have time, his roommate had pressured him into coming, saying that the others would think he was stuck up if he didn't come. As Charles enters the lounge, he looks for a place to sit, telling himself to find a seat where he can go unnoticed. Spotting a chair by the far wall near his roommate, Charles slowly makes his way around the group and gingerly sits down. During the game, the guys cheer, joke around, throw popcorn, and drink cokes. Extremely uncomfortable with the rowdy behavior, Charles tells himself that he is pathetic and just doesn't fit in. He also reminds himself to be careful not to do anything to draw attention to himself. Sitting rigidly in his chair, he looks neither left nor right but stares at the television as though to give the impression that he is intently involved. But Charles sees little of the game, his mind busy chastising himself for coming and telling himself that this has been a mistake he won't repeat. The longer the game goes on, the worse he feels, until he is absolutely devastated. Knowing how it feels to be teased unmercifully, Charles winces when he hears his friends do it to each other. He feels a sense of terror at the thought that they might focus on him for being so quiet. He wills the game to be over. When the game does finally end, Charles quickly makes his way around the group and returns to his floor in the dorm. Not wanting to see his roommate, however, he goes into the restroom, enters a stall, and sits holding his head in his hands. Trying to calm down, he remains there for 10 minutes asking himself how he will ever make it through college. Finally, emotionally exhausted, he decides to go back to his room and take a nap. Barely able to hold his head up, he walks down the hallway, praying he won't meet anyone who was in the lounge earlier. Two hours later Charles's roommate returns to find Charles waking up from a long nap. Concerned, he asks Charles if he is okay, embarrassing Charles even further. Charles tries to smile and weakly says, "Sure. I was just really tired today." His roommate, knowing something went wrong, says to Charles, "Don't let those guys bother you. They can get a little rowdy and obnoxious at times; they just think it's all part of having a good time."

2C-1. In the scenario above, underline the ideas or events that might create anxiety or fear in a person with low self-esteem or that depict behavior associated with LSE and not with healthy self-esteem. For example, watching the game with a group of guys "most of whom he doesn't know" would create anxiety for many people; those with moderate to severe LSE feel unsure of themselves when surrounded by strangers. "Though he pleaded that he didn't have time" indicates that Charles wanted to get out of the gathering. Closely examining each sentence, underline any other words or phrases that you think represent issues that could create anxiety in Charles or might be the result of anxiety from his self-talk. Again, don't worry about your decisions. No one is looking over your shoulder or evaluating what you do. This is just practice in increasing your awareness of how LSE affects us.

Once you have underlined the words and phrases in the scenario above, answer the following:
- How many phrases did you underline? _____
- Of those you underlined, how many do you think would impact individuals with healthy self-esteem? _____
- Circle the events or ideas that you think would impact those with healthy self-esteem.

2C-2. Now, look at the specific things Charles said to himself during and after the game and imagine what else he likely said to himself throughout the afternoon. Knowing that he resisted going to the football party, what do you think he thought when he finally agreed to go? For example, do you think he was criticizing himself for agreeing to do so? Do you think he was conjuring up the negative things that might happen? Put yourself in Charles's shoes and write down any additional statements he might have made to himself. Remember Charles has low self-esteem and is obviously unsure of himself in social situations. Write down both positive and negative statements that you think he might have said to himself. For instance, do you think he said that it felt good to know that his roommate was including him?

List any additional positive and negative statements that you think Charles might have said to himself during the day. Remember, we talk to ourselves constantly all day, so he probably said much more than is written above.

- When he pleads with his roommate that he doesn't have time to watch the game:

_____

_____

_____

- As he looks for a seat and then sees his roommate:

_____

_____

_____

_____

- As he makes his way to sit down:

_____

_____

_____

_____

- During the rowdy behavior:

_____

_____

_____

_____

- As he witnesses the guys teasing each other:

_____

_____

_____

_____

- As he tries to avoid drawing attention to himself:

_____

_____

_____

_____

- When the game is finally over:

_____

_____

_____

_____

- When he sits in the stall in the bathroom:

_____

_____

_____

_____

- When his roommate makes comments showing that he recognizes how uncomfortable Charles has been that afternoon:

_____

_____

_____

_____

2C-3. Look again at the self-statements that you listed above
- How many did you list? _____
- How many of them were negative? _____
- How many were positive? _____

LSE sufferers often feel overly vulnerable and at risk in situations where those with healthy self-esteem see no particular threat. This is the norm for people with LSE. All people with low self-esteem feel this way in certain situations. Consequently, they become their own worst enemies, feeding themselves distorted, irrational, negative thoughts about how poorly they are performing or how negatively others are perceiving them. (People with healthy self-esteem give themselves positive feedback, instead, which lowers their anxiety and frees them to be themselves and to appear more spontaneous and comfortable.) Those with LSE are not only imprisoned by their low self-esteem and the negative self-talk that naturally accompanies it, but they are also disabled, powerless to alter the negative feedback, unable to remove it from their thoughts, and unable to see it as anything but the truth.

2C-4. Using the Feelings List (pages 16-17), select three words that best describe what you think that Charles was *feeling* as he made the imagined self-statements in exercise 2B-2 above. You may choose to use words or phrases that are not on the list.

- When he pleads with his roommate that he doesn't have time to watch the game:

  _____

  _____

  _____

- As he looks for a seat and spots his roommate:

  _____

  _____

  _____

- As he makes his way to sit down:

  _____

  _____

  _____

- During the rowdy behavior:

  _____

  _____

  _____

- As he witnesses the guys teasing each other:

  _____

  _____

  _____

- As he tries to avoid drawing attention to himself:

  _____

  _____

  _____

- When the game is over:

  _____

  _____

  _____

- While he sits in the stall in the bathroom:

  _____

  _____

  _____

- When his roommate's shows that he recognized how uncomfortable Charles was:

  _____

  _____

  _____

Do you see how Charles's low self-esteem, his basic insecurities, and his self-doubt create his negative thoughts? Do you see how Charles's negative thoughts lead to his negative feelings and how the vicious cycle continues to create even more anxiety, nearly paralyzing him?

2C-5. Now, imagine a different Charles in the scenario above. Picture a young man who has healthy self-esteem, who likes himself, who is gregarious and outgoing, who enjoys meeting new people, who is confident that he can interact and fit in with most anyone he meets. Picture a college student who can join in with others when they are having fun and who can give and take casual teasing without being threatened or feeling attacked.

With this in mind, rewrite the scenario, omitting or altering the words or phrases that you think would be different while leaving the basic story intact. Take your time. Examine each word, phrase, and sentence, imagining what Charles would be thinking, what he would be doing and saying if he had healthy self-esteem. Begin now to rewrite the scenario.

_____

_____

_____

_____

_____

_____

_____

_____

_____

_____

_____

_____

_____

_____

_____

_____

_____

_____

Charles's self-talk creates self-doubt thereby fueling his negative feelings and effecting his attitudes and his behavior. Charles would be a much different person if he could alter his self-talk; he would be less tense in new situations, more at ease with strangers, more confident about fitting in, and less fearful in general.

 *Please go forward to **Obstacle 3, "Establishing the Source of Your LSE"** (page 122 in this book) and work through page 132. Instructions on page 132 will tell you where to go next.*

Obstacle 2, Excursion D

Successful in Work but Lacking in Relationship Skills

Pleased to know that the firm's new lawyer is an attractive, sharp, single female, Garret indulges in wishful thinking. As quickly as these thoughts surface, however, he also dismisses any notion that he might get to know her beyond the workplace. A handsome, well-dressed man himself, Garret wishes he had the courage to suggest coffee or to invite her to dinner. But he reminds himself how tongue-tied he gets in one-on-one social settings where he doesn't know how to keep up his part of the conversation. Because Garret is a high-powered defense attorney who is articulate in the courtroom and verbose when it comes to talking about the law, politics, and sports, few people would ever believe that he has difficulty communicating with women in social settings. In court, he is in his element: he's smooth, eloquent, and convincing, When talking about his other interests about which he is well-informed, he has much to say, and others often look to him for his expertise. Get him out of his element or areas of expertise, however, and Garret is a communication cripple. Insecure and uncertain of how to build a relationship and sorely lacking in social skills, Garret has become a workaholic, playing it safe by spending his time where he is most comfortable: at his work. While this single-mindedness has served him well and he has become successful and highly respected, it has also prevented him from developing skills in the area of his life that is the least refined. An overachiever as the result of his LSE, Garret hides behind his accomplishments and status. As he climbs the ladder of success, however, he remains alone and lonely. Days go by and he sees other single men talking and laughing with the new female lawyer, and he yearns to do the same. When he meets her in the hall and he feels she may, in fact, be attracted to him, he reminds himself of his proven inadequacy in relationships and sadly tells himself, "Forget it; she's out of my league. I wouldn't have the slightest idea of how to win over a woman like that and as soon as she spent time with me, she'd realize it too."

2D-1. Go back to Garret's story and underline the words or phrases that are indications or symptoms of low self-esteem, phrases that would be incompatible with the behavior or thinking of a person with healthy self-esteem.

2D-2. Notice how Garret talks himself out of the things he wants most. List the phrases, sentences or words that demonstrate the self-defeating behaviors, thoughts, and actions in this story.

_____

_____

_____

_____

_____

_____

_____

_____

_____

_____

_____

_____

_____

_____

Sadly, people who suffer from low self-esteem deny themselves the opportunity to achieve, to attain, and to participate in what they most want and most would like to do; and self-talk, not past experience, is the reason. Their low self-esteem developed in childhood as the result of messages they received from the environment in which they were born. However, it is the self-talk that nurtures and maintains these distorted, negative beliefs even in the face of facts that dispute them. In other words, a person may have proven herself to be competent, worthy, lovable, deserving, etc., but still not *feel* those things because her self-talk is based on an old videotape that has not been updated to reflect who she is today.

2D-3. Looking again at Garret's story, imagine the specific, negative self-statements Garret might be making to himself at each point. Take your time, working through the situation phrase by phrase. On the lines below, write down as many negative self-statements as you can imagine him making.

_____

_____

_____

_____

_____

_____

_____

_____

_____

_____

_____

_____

_____

2D-4. Now, taking the self-statements you have written *one by one*, select words from the Feelings List that you think would best describe how Garret feels following each negative self-statement. Feel free to use phrases or words that are not on the list.

_____

_____

_____

_____

_____

_____

_____

_____

_____

_____

_____

_____

_____

2D-5. One by one, looking at each negative statement you listed in 2D-3, rephrase the statement in a way that would not be self-defeating or discouraging. For example, if you think Garret was saying to himself, "What an attractive new addition to our firm. Too bad I don't know how to make a play for her. Too bad I'm such a retard when it comes to women," you might rephrase that self-statement to say, "Hey, its great having an attractive new partner like Sara. She's very sharp and I think I'll try to get to know her. I'm a nice guy and have some good qualities. Hopefully we will like each other. I'm not as smooth socially as I am in the courtroom, but that will come with practice. I'll be friendly and see how it goes." This is not to suggest that Garret should fabricate or tell himself things that are not true, but rather that he should be more factual about his self-statements rather than choosing to constantly feed himself statements that are only negative and that are not fully based on fact.

Now you try it. First, copy the negative statement and then rephrase it so it is not self-defeating. Then move on to the next negative statement you find. If you have difficulty with this exercise, remember this is just practice. It will become easier over time.

_____

_____

_____

_____

_____

_____

_____

_____

_____

_____

_____

_____

_____

_____

_____

_____

_____

_____

_____

2D-6. Focusing on the new, positive statements you have written in 2D-5, go to the Feelings List and choose words that you think would describe how Garret would have felt if he had said these more positive statements to himself, rather than the negative ones in the original scenario. Write these words next to the statements in 2D-5. You may want to use a different color of ink. Feel free to use words from the Feelings List or to choose words or phrases of your own.

Can you see a difference in how Garret would feel about himself if his self-statements were based solely on fact and his current history rather than on negative conclusions that he drew in childhood? For instance: he is successful as an attorney, meaning he is fully capable of leaning new skills; he is "smooth, eloquent, and convincing" indicating that he knows some basic communication techniques; he is respected by others, which shows that he must not have any apparent faults that would immediately prevent him from initiating social contact; and he is well-informed, which might suggest that he would have something of interest to talk about.

Can you see how Garret would feel and how his confidence would be elevated in the area of relationship-building if he were able to see that as a successful attorney, he has gained skills that are valuable in relationship-building and that he is fully capable of learning additional skills?

Isn't it likely that Garret would be less cautious and more willing to initiate a friendship with Sara if he were making encouraging and supportive self-statements based on the above facts rather than continuing to berate himself and to focus on the worst possible outcome?

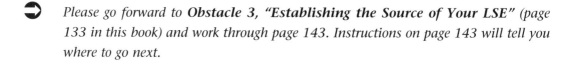

*Please go forward to **Obstacle 3, "Establishing the Source of Your LSE"** (page 133 in this book) and work through page 143. Instructions on page 143 will tell you where to go next.*

Obstacle 2, Excursion E

Independent and Talented But Vulnerable and Fearful

Molly works as an auto mechanic in an all-woman auto repair shop, but her true love is painting. Her dream is to eventually paint full-time. During the day, Molly works on carburetors and distributors, but two evenings a week she takes art classes. On weekends she usually drives into the country or to small communities to find nostalgic material for her paintings. In the beginning Molly began painting as a way to fill her time since she lives alone and has no close friends. Realizing over time that she was a creative and talented painter with an eye for detail and a steady hand, her painting has filled her empty life—at least, until lately.

Several weeks ago, Molly's art instructor asked her to stay after class and shared with her that he was opening a new gallery within the month. He then said that he thought her work was excellent and saleable and that when she had completed a few pieces, he would like to arrange a showing of her work. Molly was both elated and terrified. While this had been her dream, she felt immediately queasy. Only later did she realize that she feared what it would be like to have others evaluate her work. She liked what she painted as did some of the other students, but she had never shown her work to family members or friends, fearful of their responses. As it was, Molly's family ridiculed her for being a mechanic, especially her brothers who openly made snide remarks about her need to compete with men. She knew that even her father disapproved. Certainly she could not expect support from her family in anything else she did; the men didn't seem to place much value on women except when the women were doing something for them.

*Molly enjoys her work as a mechanic; it fits with her need to analyze and figure things out, **and** it enables her to avoid contact and involvement with people. Now, her art instructor is suggesting she put her creative abilities on display where she will be exposed and the recipient of scrutiny. Feeling vulnerable and nearly paralyzed by fear, Molly begins withdrawing from her painting, even skipping two weeks of art class.*

Most people, especially those with low self-esteem, are not aware of the negative tapes they carry with them. They are not conscious that the fear and anxiety they experience is due more to the replaying of these tapes than to the actual situation they are presently encountering. Molly's fear, for instance, entirely originates from the treatment she received from her family. Though she is now successful as a mechanic and has received positive feedback and raises at the shop, Molly still sees herself and her accomplishments as inferior. Compared to the amount of criticism she received through her formative years, Molly has received relatively little affirmation, mainly because she is isolated and avoids feedback. When she has received praise at work or from her art teacher, she temporarily enjoys the feeling but soon finds a way to discount it. Now when faced with the possibility of placing her work on display for the general public, Molly has no way of discerning the difference between how a talented artist will be viewed by art patrons and how her family responded to her in the past. Coupled with her self-doubt about her ability, which creates so much anguish for her, she begins to avoid her creative work, thereby temporarily relieving her anxiety and performing the perfect self-sabotage of denying herself what she most wants: validation and affirmation of her worth.

The scenario above is typical of the way LSE sufferers act out self-defeating behaviors when faced with situations they see as traumatic, especially when they fill their heads with painful memories and messages from the past. Thus, given an opportunity that might be in their best interest or that they would really like to do, their videotape reminds them of similar past events and the negative feedback or treatment they received. Often they are unable to visualize a different or better outcome, because like Molly, they have avoided situations where they might have experienced different types of interactions and relationships with healthier people.

2E-1. With all this in mind, reread Molly's story. Slowly look at each sentence and imagine how Molly feels. Then write down the specific self-statements that you think Molly might have made at each point of her story, both positive and negative. Allow yourself time to try to put yourself in her place and write as many as you can think of. For example, after her art teacher spoke with her, do you think she said, "Oh, no, I couldn't handle people criticizing my pieces," or "No one will like my work—I'm not good enough yet to try to sell my work," or "He's just wanting art work to fill his gallery; he probably doesn't think I'm that good." What do you think a person with low self-esteem who's come from a critical and disapproving background might say to herself?

_____

_____

_____

_____

_____

_____

_____

_____

_____

_____

_____

_____

2E-2. Now, using the Feelings List, choose one or more words for each of the above self-statements and add them to 2E-1.

2E.3. How would Molly's feelings be different if the feedback she gave herself was primarily based on who she is today and the skills she has attained?

_____

_____

_____

_____

_____

_____

➲   *Before continuing, please read **Chapter 6, "Listening to and Controlling Our Inner Voice"** of **Breaking the Chain of Low Self-Esteem** (pages 167-186).*

*When you have finished reading Chapter 6 go forward to **Obstacle 3, "Establishing the Source of Your LSE"** (page 144 in this book) and work through page 153, where more instructions await you.*

Intro to Obstacle 2: Excursions F, G, H, J

Recognizing Our Own Self-Sabotaging Behaviors

This next segment is essential to the ultimate establishment and maintenance of a healthy self-esteem. In the previous excursions, you were asked to focus on the actions, thoughts, and feelings of others who suffer from low self-esteem. Sometimes it is easier to see self-defeating behaviors in others than in ourselves; because we have no personal attachment to that situation, our own emotions are not involved. When our own actions or responses are the target of analysis, however, our ability to be objective is thwarted by the weighty and cumbersome baggage we carry—baggage full-to-bursting with fear and anxiety associated with negative memories of similar incidents, and the distorted conclusions we have drawn as a result of the inaccurate and painful messages we have received. Consequently, when we are in situations like those just examined, our perspective is clouded; often when we look at our own dilemmas, we feel we have no choice—or had no choice in the past—other than to succumb to the fear, acting in such a way as to protect ourselves from further pain and humiliation. However, having now looked at the self-sabotaging behaviors, thinking, and feelings of others, you are probably more able to objectively recognize the process of self-destruction that accompanies LSE.

With developing awareness of how our inaccurate tapes influence our daily thinking, including our perceptions of others, our interpretation of the behavior of others toward us, our opinions, our reactions, our view of our own performance and abilities, our hope for the future and our words and behavior, we make progress on our journey toward recovery. In other words, the more mindful we become of the frequent ways in which we are sabotaging ourselves again and again through inaccurate thoughts and interpretations, the clearer will be our journey. Thus we strive to dismantle this pattern of irrational thinking, analyzing it for its basis in truth or duplicity, then overhauling this unhealthy habit of irrational thinking by replacing it with reasoning that is founded not on emotion, assumptions, or a distorted tape, but on accurate information and analysis based solely on fact and history.

It is of the utmost importance that you do not attempt to measure your progress in this journey in the way you would count miles left to travel on an ordinary trip, for recovery is not so specific or predictable as estimating how many hours it would take to drive from Seattle to San Francisco. Plus, while this workbook is the "full-meal deal," the whole of what you need to know to overcome LSE, the principles here cannot be consumed at one sitting, like a banquet. Instead, results will come with your accumulation of awareness and information over time, with developing skills from hours of practice, and with the growing hope and confidence gained from many small successes. Once you have thoroughly digested it, you will begin to experience the benefits of this program of recovery that has proven successful, unmatched in its effectiveness, and life-altering for those who follow and practice the prescribed guidelines and suggestions. Continue on. Be hopeful. Be diligent.

Self-sabotage in all areas of life

The life of every person who suffers from low self-esteem is affected by his LSE. Whether he has avoided relationships or is unsuccessful in relationships, has excelled through workaholic tendencies or never fully developed a thriving career, whether he has become highly educated or avoided it, his low self-esteem has in some way destructively influenced his decisions in some part of his life. Consequently, becoming aware of our fear and our anxiety and how they drive us in one direction or another in our decision-making is very important to recognizing the hurdles before us and to establishing a strategy to remove them. As you work though this workbook, your self-sabotaging behaviors will come to light, your self-defeating patterns will be exposed, and you will understand the reasons for this behavior. This understanding alone will open the doors to change and recovery and that will only be the beginning. For as you recognize why you do what you do, you will also see that other options are available and that you can make other choices which can help you succeed in getting and doing what you really want. The following are examples of times and ways that people with LSE have engaged in self-sabotaging behavior.

REMEMBER: *A self-sabotage is any situation in which by your own behavior, you deny yourself the very thing you want most, whether it be the opportunity to engage in an activity, to be with others and form relationships, or to enhance your life in some other way.*

- *Meg is invited to join a group of six other women who meet to read and discuss books twice a month. Though Meg loves to read, is available on the night they meet, and thinks it would be great to be a part of the group, she declines the offer because she is fearful that she wouldn't have anything to contribute and would look dumb.*

- *Jarred is lonely, and while he admires several of his coworkers from afar, he makes no effort to try to get to know any of them because he feels he has nothing to offer and would not know how to converse with them.*

- *Betsy feels that she has some very good ideas that would increase the efficiency of her office, but when given the opportunity by her manager to offer suggestions for change, she doesn't speak up and share her thoughts, even though she realizes that doing so would probably enhance her possibility for a promotion.*

- *Knowing that the salaries at his firm far exceed what his brother-in-law Russell is now getting at his job and aware that Russell is highly skilled, Tom encourages his boss to make Russell an immediate offer for an open position. Later that week when Tom's boss calls to offer him the job, Russell is surprised and immediately filled with fear and trepidation. "What if I am not able to handle the position? Tom and everyone in the family would know." Russell, who has been at the same job for 14 years, has never looked for a better job and has resigned himself that this is the best he can do. Now faced with an unsolicited opportunity but one Russell views as potentially devastating, he tries to think of any reasonable excuse for refusing the offer.*

- *Luke wishes he had a better job and each quarter he looks at the community college catalogs that come in the mail, thinking he should take some classes and maybe even get a degree. As he browses through the bulletins, however, his anxiety begins to grow and he hears his father telling him he was stupid, worthless, lazy, an idiot, unfit—anything that came to his mind when he'd been drinking. Luke also remembers his painful high school days, times when he was so timid and fearful that he was unable to participate in class or ask for the help he needed. After an hour, Luke concludes that he is probably doing the best he can and tosses the catalog in the trash.*

- *While her family and friends admire Kattarina's achievements (at 33 she is an executive for a well-known pharmaceutical firm), they worry about her lack of social life and wonder why she works so hard rather than making time for relationships. Of course, they are unaware that Kattarina has become this successful as a direct result of her low self-esteem; that her need to prove herself as adequate has stimulated her relentless pursuit of success and, ultimately, of respect. Unsure how to deal with people on a social level, Kattarina has sought education and then has devoted herself entirely to advancing her career, an arena where knowing what is expected is much more apparent than in relationships. Unfortunately, because Kattarina devoted most of her time to her career, she has avoided developing social skills and now feels more inadequate than ever. Thus, her success in one realm has become her failure in another.*

- *Maitlin is divorced and the mother and primary custodian of three children. While wanting to be a better parent than her own parents were, she is so overwhelmed with her circumstances and with uncertainty about what to do differently that she does nothing to learn appropriate parenting skills or to improve her own low self-esteem. As is typical of those with LSE, she does what she knows and has learned, repeating the cycle of being overly critical and demanding of her children, creating in them the same feelings of inadequacy and lack of worth that have molded her life.*

- *Kari tolerates her husband's critical and controlling behavior because she is fearful that confronting him might ultimately cause the end of the relationship, an event that would leave her alone and unable to cope with life's demands and people's expectations. Kari's low self-esteem has created a dependence on others and has further entrenched her lack of self-reliance and fear of the world. If she chooses to stay with her husband, she will continue to feel safe but also manipulated and dominated, further eroding her self-esteem. So far, her fear and anxiety have prevented her from leaving.*

- *Attractive and outgoing, Sierra has had many romantic relationships but has been unable to maintain them. Full of self-doubt, she finds it hard to trust a partner who professes to care about her; determined to find out, she sets up situations that test whether these declarations are true. For instance, she has purposely and routinely asked her partners to do things for her that require extra effort to see if they willingly agree to do so. She has also closely scrutinized the things they say to her, how much time they want to be with her, and how much money they spend on her, frequently confronting them when she is disappointed. Quality partners have left her because they could not tolerate this behavior.*

- *Riley is 39, single, alone, and without friends. Unaware of how to build and maintain relationships, he tries to get people to like him by doing things for them. He readily volunteers to loan them his truck or to haul things for them and will never take money, even for gas. People are grateful but don't find this to be the basis of a substantial relationship, which Riley doesn't understand. Riley never initiates activities with others because he has been turned down in the past and fears more rejection. In addition, he is fearful of saying the wrong thing, so he seldom shares an opinion, an idea, or a perception. In fact, he reveals very little about his thoughts and even less about his feelings. He usually accepts invitations to the homes of others but never reciprocates because he is too fearful to play host. While he is a nice person, there is nothing unique about Riley that would attract people to him or that would develop into a deep friendship.*

In these examples, the individuals chose self-sabotaging paths, opting for the familiar rather than taking chances on the unknown, unable to believe they might be deserving and worthy of success. Consequently, they continue to experience unfulfilled lives because of the fear and anxiety that accompany low self-esteem. Though this choice is painful, they could have made different choices—and continued to choose—on the basis of what they thought would bring the best results over time rather than deciding what felt most comfortable at the moment. However, being ruled by negative thoughts and memories (whether accurately interpreted or not) that are too excruciating to ignore, they have relied on emotion rather than rational thought as the deciding factor.

➲   *Please continue to page 65 and work through page 69 where more instructions await you.*

Obstacle 2, Excursion F

Working Through an Incident of Self-sabotage

Take a few minutes to focus on a difficult past event in your life, a time when you were upset. While this may be painful, attempt to recall your experience. Think about what happened and who was involved. Think about what you said to yourself and how you felt. Were you embarrassed? Did you feel rejected? Did you think others were responding to you in some strange way, perceiving you negatively, or treating you with a lack of respect? Think about what you did as a result of how you felt.

Below, you are asked to describe five of these situations. Notice the ways in which what you did or said proved to be self-sabotaging; in other words, notice where your behavior avoided, eliminated, or in some other way sabotaged an opportunity that you might have had. For each incident, describe:

- exactly what happened
- the significance of the situation
- what you began to say to yourself immediately following the incident
- what you felt
- how you responded in words or actions
- what the final outcome of the situation was
- what you said to yourself when the incident was over
- how you felt about yourself when it was behind you

2F-1. With as much detail as you think is important, describe one of these incidents, sharing the significance of it and who was involved, e.g., "My boss told me he wanted to see me in his office right away" or "A coworker whom I admired asked me out to lunch for the first time" or "Coworkers asked me to join them for drinks after work on Friday. I have turned down these invitations in the past so that my coworkers wouldn't see how awkward I am in such settings." (Note that the situation may be a perfectly natural or normal one that would not cause undue anxiety for someone with healthy self-esteem.)

_____

_____

_____

_____

_____

_____

_____

2F-2. The first thing that occurs in such an incident for the LSE sufferer is that our self-esteem is threatened. When that happens, we experience an emotional reaction far out of proportion to the incident itself because we are reacting to the sum of our negative doubts. We realize we are in danger of revealing our inadequacies or have already done so and we become irrational, imagining that worst-case scenarios have happened or are about to happen. We imagine that the boss is going to fire us or that if we go to lunch with the admired coworker, he will see our inadequacies and will never want to lunch with us again, or worse yet, he might say negative things to other coworkers about us.

• What were your immediate feelings in the incident you described in 2F-1? Use the Feelings List or choose words of your own.

_____

_____

_____

2F-3. Once our low self-esteem—our self-doubt—is re-activated, we begin to talk negatively to ourselves. Whether or not we are aware of it, we automatically begin to berate ourselves and/or others, and we think that the worst has happened or is about to. Becoming aware of these self-statements before we act on them is the task now at hand; developing this awareness of how you talk to yourself is a big leap toward reaching your destination.

Even though self-statements cause our feelings, it's much more difficult to identify those self-statements than the feelings that result from them because the emotional reaction is so instantaneous; it hardly seems that any thoughts preceded them. That's why you were asked to share your feelings first and then to work backwards from them. Now try to imagine your self-talk:

• What might you have been saying to yourself as soon as the incident in 2F-1 happened? Did you instantly begin to doubt that you could handle the situation?

_____

_____

_____

_____

_____

_____

_____

_____

_____

_____

_____

It is at this point that the LSE sufferer acts out of fear, often doing and saying things that are not in our own best interest. We have given ourselves critical messages; our emotions are running full bore, and we feel extremely frightened, possibly to the point of terror.

Our next thought is for self-protection: what can we do to feel safe? This might mean leaving the premises, (going to the bathroom where no one will be watching us, feigning sickness and going home, etc.), lying to get out of the lunch, reacting defensively or angrily, or anything else we can do to protect ourselves immediately from what we consider to be imminent danger

At this point, we are usually so consumed with the emotions we are experiencing that we are unable to take a step back and recognize the process that is taking place. Thus, the goal is to learn how to remain objective and rational, realizing that an incident has occurred that seems threatening and has activated our low self-esteem. Secondly recognizing that this activation is causing us to reinstate our habit of critical self-talk, which, if left unbridled will upset our emotional equilibrium and result in self-defeating behavior. In other words, the goal is to stop the downhill slide into irrational, excessive, and self-defeating behaviors by eliminating false assumptions and inaccurate conclusions and only allowing self-statements that are rational and true.

2F-4. With this in mind, describe your actions following the incident in 2F-1:

- What did you actually do? Did you become depressed or so consumed with worry about meeting with the boss that you couldn't enjoy your lunch or couldn't focus on conversations going on around you? Did you turn down the lunch with the coworker by making some excuse?

_____

_____

_____

_____

_____

_____

_____

_____

2F-5. How did the situation work out? For instance, was the meeting with the boss as bad as you had anticipated? Was he really upset with you? Regardless of his reasons for asking you to meet with him, how did you act and feel during the meeting? Or if you went to lunch with the coworker, how was the experience?

_____

_____

_____

_____

_____

_____

_____

_____

2F-6. What did you say to yourself when the incident was over? Did you berate or chide yourself, did you label your behavior in negative terms, or did you compliment yourself, telling yourself you handled the situation well? Write down as many self-statements as you can remember or imagine what you probably said to yourself.

_____

_____

_____

_____

_____

_____

_____

_____

2F-7. Select words from the Feelings List that best describe how you felt when the event was over. Were you pleased with your reactions and your behavior? Were you relieved that the situation was over? Were you depressed or disappointed in yourself?

_____

_____

_____

2F-8. How long did these residual feelings last? Was it minutes, hours, days, or even weeks?

_____

_____

➲   *Before continuing, please read **Chapter 8,** (pages 213-233), **"The Relentless Pursuit of Validation"** of **Breaking the Chain of Low Self-Esteem**. Then return to this page and work through page 72.*

Obstacle 2, Excursion G

A Second Incident of Self-sabotage

2G-1. Describe another incident, sharing its significance, who was involved, the importance of those involved, e.g., supervisor, school advisor, parent, significant other, policeman, neighbor. (Note again that the situation you describe may be a perfectly normal situation that would not cause undue anxiety for those with healthy self-esteem. This explains why others may not understand your response to this or other similar situations.)

_____

_____

_____

_____

_____

_____

_____

_____

_____

2G-2. What were your immediate feelings? Refer to the Feelings List for help.

_____

_____

_____

REMEMBER: Self-talk precedes feelings, but until we develop awareness of our self-statements, we are likely to recognize our feelings first.

2G-3. What negative statements did you immediately begin to make to yourself?

_____

_____

_____

_____

_____

_____

_____

_____

2G-4. What did you actually do? Did you worry excessively so that it interfered with your day? Did you flee from the situation, stay home, avoid contact with others? Or did you lash out, say things you wish you hadn't, or in some other way embarrass yourself?

_____

_____

_____

_____

_____

_____

2G-5. How did the situation work out? Did you accept the invitation, confront the person who hurt your feelings, or return the damaged article to the store where you bought it?

_____

_____

_____

_____

_____

_____

_____

_____

2G-6. What did you say to yourself when the incident was over? Did you berate or chide yourself, did you label your behavior in negative terms, or did you compliment

yourself, telling yourself you handled the situation well? Write down as many statements as you can remember or imagine what you probably said to yourself.

_____

_____

_____

_____

_____

_____

_____

_____

2G-7. Select words from the Feelings List that best describe how you felt when the
event was over. Were you pleased with your reactions and your behavior? Were
you relieved that the situation was over? Were you depressed or disappointed in
yourself?

_____

_____

_____

2G-8. How long did these residual feelings last? Was it minutes, hours, days, or even
weeks?

_____

_____

➲   *Please go forward to **Obstacle 3, "Establishing the Source of Your LSE"** (page
162 in this book) and work through page 183. Instructions on page 183 will tell you
where to go next.*

Obstacle 2, Excursion H

A Third Incident of Self-sabotage

2H-1. Describe another incident you have experienced that in someway caused you grief, sharing its significance and who was involved, and the role of those involved. Only through practice will your self-statements become more obvious. (Again, note that the situation may be a perfectly natural situation that might not cause undue anxiety for those with healthy self-esteem.)

2H-2. What were your immediate feelings? Refer to the Feelings List for help.

2H-3. What negative self-statements did you immediately begin making?

_____

_____

_____

2H-4. What did you actually do? How did you deal with the incident that upset you?

_____

_____

_____

_____

_____

_____

2H-5. How did the situation work out?

_____

_____

_____

_____

_____

_____

2H-6. What did you say to yourself when the incident was over? Write down as many statements as you can remember or imagine that you would said to yourself.

_____

_____

_____

_____

_____

_____

_____

_____

2H-7. Select words from the Feelings List that best describe how you felt when the event was over.

_____

_____

_____

2H-8. How long did these residual feelings last? Was it minutes, hours, days, or even weeks?

_____

_____

 *Please go forward to **Obstacle 4, "Catching Up"** (page 274 in this book) and work through page 276. Instructions on page 276 will tell you where to go next.*

Obstacle 2, Excursion J

The Fourth Incident of Self-sabotage

2J-1. Describe a fourth incident, sharing its importance, who was involved, and the significance of those involved.

_____

_____

_____

_____

_____

_____

_____

_____

_____

2J-2. What were your immediate feelings? Refer to the Feelings List for ideas.

_____

_____

_____

2J-3. What self-statements did you immediately begin making?

_____

_____

_____

_____

_____

_____

_____

2J-4. What did you actually do?

_____

_____

_____

_____

_____

_____

_____

_____

2J-5. How did the situation work out?

_____

_____

_____

_____

_____

_____

2J-6. What did you say to yourself when the incident was over?

_____

_____

_____

_____

_____

_____

_____

2J-7. Select words from the Feelings List that best describe how you felt when the event
       was over.

_____

_____

_____

_____

2J-8. How long did these residual feelings last? Was it minutes, hours, days, or even weeks?

_____

_____

The exercises you have just completed are developing your self-awareness so that you can see how often you talk to yourself, how frequently your self-talk is negative, and how your self-talk affects your feelings and actions. You may also be beginning to see that your self-talk is what maintains your low self-esteem and that it sets the stage for the self-sabotaging that we all do when we have acquired low self-esteem.

➲   *Before proceeding, please read **Chapter 7, "The Search for Unconditional Love"** (pages 191-211) of **Breaking the Chain of Low Self-Esteem**.*

*When you have finished with chapter 7, go to **Obstacle 3: "Establishing the Source of your LSE,"** (page 197 in this book) and work through page 217. On page 217 instructions will tell you where to go next.*

Intro to: Obstacle 2, Excursions K, L, M, N

Recognizing the Scars of our Dysfunctional Backgrounds and Dismantling Our Negative Thoughts

Critical to the recovery journey is the process of first becoming aware of—and then examining—the negative self-statements that control our lives. We must analyze everything we say for its degree of rationality or truthfulness; in other words, we must learn to decipher the things we are telling ourselves for their truth and their historical fact. In trying to get to the truth, we must be aware of the stumbling blocks that get in our way:

Past hurts have formed scars—memories that become barriers to future growth. Among these stumbling blocks are:

1. *our inability to recognize that any incident can be interpreted in many different ways—* that the way we see ourselves is not necessarily the way others see us and that our interpretation of their intentions may not be accurate
2. *our rigidity and inability to consider options or be open to change*
3. *our deep sensitivity which causes us to easily be wounded and to expect the worst from others*

Consequently, LSE sufferers often become their own worst enemies while being totally unaware they are doing so. The following excursions delve into some of the ways that people sabotage themselves and will help develop awareness of how we can fall into these patterns of behavior.

Obstacle 2, Excursion K

People have different perceptions.

Shaped by what we have been told, what we have seen, and what we have learned, we each have a view that is ours alone. This assessment may not vary greatly from the perception of someone we know well or it may be all together different from someone else's, *but it will never be exactly the same in every aspect.* Those of us with low self-esteem have an especially unique perspective because we base our views on the level of threat we think is present, and often we perceive events and situations as frightening and potentially dangerous to our emotional stability. We are especially reluctant to become involved in unfamiliar situations where we don't know what is expected of us or where we might feel inadequate or out of place. Those with healthy self-esteem do not share this view; some with healthy self-esteem might view participation in a new event as exciting, others might see it as boring, still others as a waste of time, but the difference being that those with healthy self-esteem would not likely be frightened by the situation. Rather they base their decisions or opinions on what they want, what they like, and what they think or believe, whereas people with LSE base their decisions on fear of failure, fear of rejection or feelings of devastation, and fear of other present or future negative consequences.

Thus:
- If Harry is asked to attend a party, his response will largely depend on how he feels about himself. If Harry has healthy self-esteem, he will choose to go or not go based on whether he is busy, whether he is tired or feeling energetic, whether he wants to be with those who will likely be at the party, and whether or not he likes parties. If Harry has moderate to severe LSE, however, he will make his choice on how anxious he will be beforehand and how threatened he thinks he will feel once he gets there.

- If Tom's boss chews him out for coming late to work too often, Tom may over-react defensively if he has low self-esteem. Feeling that the boss is telling him he is a "bad" person, Tom may make excuses, blame others, and even lie about coming late. Devastated by the reprimand, Tom may also remain quiet and begin telling himself that the boss just doesn't like him or that his job is in jeopardy.

Later he may become very depressed. If Tom has healthy self-esteem and is an honest person, he will just admit that it's true and tell his boss that he will do better. He won't make the situation bigger than it is, he won't try to find fault with the boss, and he won't try to rationalize that his tardiness shouldn't matter.

•   If Annie is asked to go bowling with her coworkers, her response will depend on how threatening she thinks the experience may be. If she has bowled before and thinks she is an above-average bowler, she will be more likely to go than if she thinks she is average or below and concludes that she will embarrass herself. Similarly, if Annie remembers previous occasions when she joined in with her coworkers and felt she didn't fit in, she is likely to be very anxious and find an excuse to refuse the invitation.

•   When offered a promotion, Kimberly becomes nervous and fearful that she will not be up to the task—that she doesn't have the skills necessary to do the job she's being offered. She tells herself that she is better off at her present job, even though the pay isn't very good, because people see her as successful there; she concludes that if she takes the new job she may not be able to do what's expected and people will then see her as a failure.

Concentrate now on your own past feelings, thinking, and behavior as it applies to the kind of examples above. Remember, the purpose of these exercises is not to force you to dwell upon past failures, but to help you learn to recognize when you are irrationally letting your LSE control and negatively affect the rest of your life.

2K-1. When and where have you let your fears control your decisions? Describe one such situation. How did you feel afterwards? Were you upset that you didn't do what you really wanted to?

_____

_____

_____

_____

_____

_____

_____

2K-2. Look now to see how you could have reacted differently. What other choices might you have made? What would you try to do differently today?

_____

_____

_____

_____

_____

_____

_____

2K-3. Can you think of times when you were not able to accept a compliment, when your mind immediately read into the kind words of others some ulterior motive or where you completely twisted the compliment and felt bad as a result? Try not to feel embarrassed—these behaviors are typical of people who suffer from low self-esteem and are not a condemnation of you as a person. Give two to three examples here.

_____

_____

_____

_____

_____

_____

_____

2K-4. Write down three things you could immediately say to a person who compliments you, Then think of three things you could say to yourself about the compliment. Then, memorize these statements so you will be prepared to use these phrases in response to a compliment. For instance, you might say to the other person, "What a nice compliment. Thank you" or "Thank you. I appreciate your kind words" or "Thanks, I like my new hair cut too." Afterwards you could say to yourself. "My hair must look pretty good. Others seem to like it" or "I guess my speech (solo, new recipe, report) was pretty good. Several people have taken he time to tell me they liked it." Don't allow yourself to say negative things to yourself that haven't been stated. For instance, don't say, "I don't think they liked my dinner" unless they say so or refuse to eat it. Don't tell yourself that your speech wasn't good, if the only comments you have received have been positive. Don't make up negative things that aren't based on truth, fact, or history.

_____

_____

_____

_____

_____

_____

_____

_____

2K-5. Have you ever felt that people were watching you more than they did others, that when people are laughing, they must be laughing at you, or that they are overly *negatively* focused on you? If so, write down one or more incidents that you remember. Did you at some later time realize that these people probably weren't that aware of you? Write about that awareness as well.

_____

_____

_____

_____

_____

_____

2K-6. People are generally not nearly as aware of our presence as we think they are. People with LSE are often fearful of eating alone in a restaurant because they are sure that everyone is watching them and thinking that they don't have friends to go to dinner with. The truth is that most people in a restaurant are focused on themselves and their companions. Write down three or four statements that you could tell yourself when you become fearful that others are watching or analyzing you.

_____

_____

_____

_____

_____

_____

_____

_____

2K-7. Do you recollect times that you have overreacted due to your low self-esteem? Write down what you remember doing; when you remember figuring out that you had overreacted; and what, if anything, you did about it (apologized, avoided the person for a time, etc.).

_____

_____

_____

_____

_____

_____

_____

_____

_____

_____

*Please go forward to **Obstacle 3, "Establishing the Source of Your LSE"** (page 218 in this book) and work through page 236. Instructions on page 236 will tell you where to go next.*

Obstacle 2, Excursion L

People with LSE are overly sensitive.

Unfortunately, when we suffer from low self-esteem, we tend to be so sensitive and fearful of rejection and failure that we read into the behavior and words of others, negative intentions, duplicitous motivation, and condemnation that often don't exist. Expecting the worst-case scenario, we actively watch for evidence that will confirm our belief that others don't love and respect us. Being able to admit that we are doing this—overreacting and reading into situations criticism or rejection that is not present—-is crucial to our recovery. Making such an admission is also a very difficult thing to do because it says that much of the misery we experience is self-inflicted. Remember, however, that these habits are typical of those who struggle because of damaged self-esteem.

In other words, a common consequence of the negative self-view of LSE is that everything we hear and observe is filtered through the perspective that we are in some way inferior or unworthy, beliefs that often lead us to project onto others these negative perceptions. In other words, because we have grown to believe that we are undeserving, we think that others believe that as well; because we have been led to think we are inadequate, we assume that others see us the same way.

As we have seen in earlier exercises, *thinking dictates feelings*, so that the way we feel is the result of what we have been telling ourselves. Whether we are aware of exactly what those self-stated messages are, we can be sure that if we feel something negative, it is the result of what we have been telling ourselves, whether or not it is based on truth.

• *When David tells Sara that he likes her new haircut, her response will depend on her level of self-esteem. If she feels good about herself, she will be pleased that he likes her hair; if she suffers from LSE, she may read more into his comment than is intended, wondering if he didn't like it before she got it cut.*

• *If Jackie walks by a group of coworkers who break out in laughter after she passes, she probably won't think much about it if she has healthy self-esteem, except to wonder what joke she missed. If she has low self-esteem, however, she will likely think that they were laughing at her.*

•   *When Jake asks Martha out for coffee, she wonders what he wants from her, why he is asking her out. Knowing that he has recently broken up with his girlfriend, she guesses that he may be using her to make the ex-girlfriend jealous. An LSE sufferer, Martha can't imagine that Jake might like her for who she is. She is sure that he must have an ulterior motive.*

2L-1. Think back to times when you realized after the fact that you had been too sensitive and read into the words or behavior of others something that was not true. For instance, when someone didn't return your phone call or email right away, did you think they were ignoring you, being rude, or didn't like you? Describe two such incidents.

_____

_____

_____

_____

_____

_____

_____

_____

2L-2. What do you think you said to yourself at the time of each incident that led to misconstruing or misreading the intentions of the other person. For instance, did you increase your anxiety by saying, "She is purposely not returning my phone call? She must not want to be friends with me"? List the specific statements you remember making to yourself at the time. Or, if you cannot remember, list the things you think you probably said to yourself.

_____

_____

_____

_____

_____

_____

A common mistake LSE sufferers make is that when they misconstrue the words, intentions or behavior of others, their negative responses tend to sprout new wings and grow. In other words, they start with one detail: "she didn't return my phone call." They misconstrue it to mean: "she doesn't like me." Then within seconds they expand the thought to include others: "I don't think Sara likes me either. She never calls or initiates anything with me." From there it builds to: "In fact, I don't have very many people I can count on."

Thus, they take one situation and expand it to encompass far more than the situation warranted. Then when they do receive a return phone call two days later, along with an apology and explanation that the person has been out of town, LSE sufferers are instantly relieved and all is forgotten. Sadly, they don't recognize that they regularly overreact and cause themselves unnecessary grief. They don't see that their basic negative view of self leads them to distorted perceptions, unreasonable doubt, and second-guessing of the words, intentions, and actions of others.

People with LSE tend to be very self-focused. If you didn't return my phone call, it says something about me and how you feel about me. They seldom consider that there could be many other reasons the person has not returned the call. Tending to "look" narcissistic, they seem to think that everything that happens or doesn't happen says something about them. Rather than check out the validity of their conclusions, they believe that if the boss is angry, they must have done something wrong. If their spouse is quiet, there must be a problem in their relationship. Such responses are typical of those with LSE. While it may feel embarrassing to admit that you are guilty of these reactions, remember that they are common manifestations of the distorted thinking that accompanies LSE.

2L-3. Referring to 2L-1, what effect do you think such statements had on you had the time? Did you begin to ruminate about how others might not like you either? Did you begin to question all of your relationships? Did you become anxious? upset? depressed?

_____

_____

_____

_____

_____

_____

2L-4. How accurate were your reaction statements? Rewrite the self-statements you think you made so that they are now truthful and factual. For instance, you could have said, "She must be busy; she'll get back to me when she has time." or "There's no reason to think she doesn't like me. We have a good time together and she often shares personal information with me."

_____

_____

_____

_____

_____

_____

➲   *Please go forward to **Obstacle 4, "Catching Up"** (page 280 in this book) and work through page 281. Instructions on page 281 will tell you where to go next.*

Obstacle 2, Excursion M

LSE can lead to rigidity.

Blake thinks men should be the boss in the home and make all the major decisions; they shouldn't have to answer to their wives for how they spend their time. He got this attitude from his father who not only ruled the roost at home, but who verbally abused Blake's mother. Blake didn't like the way his father talked to his mother, but now he treats his wife in much the same way—his third wife, that is—for Blake has been married three times and doesn't get why he can't keep a woman. In each marriage, he blames the woman when things begin to deteriorate. Blake is insecure as the result of his father's critical and dominating personality and behavior. He wants to have a lifelong relationship but has no insight about how to treat a woman, no understanding of what a relationship really is. Rather than try to get help or consider learning new ways of relating, he repeats the same behaviors, growing angry when his wife doesn't defer to him and his wishes. Blake is rigid. He has one way of doing things and is closed to even considering there might be a better way, even though he is miserable.

We must never lose sight of the fact that what we once learned but now know was wrong can be unlearned and replaced with the truth. That what we don't know but want and need to know can still be learned and made part of our reservoir of knowledge. Analyzing what we were taught for its validity and reliability is a part of the maturation process. Through the teen years and into early adulthood, each of us attempts to discover the facts, to draw conclusions, and to develop our own beliefs, whether about religion, politics, lifestyle, economics or, as in this case, our view of ourselves and how we fit into the world. And as with all such journeys of discovery, the end result largely depends on our willingness to examine many different points of view and engage in varied experiences. For many people, this is difficult. Having learned to do and think a certain way, they become rigid and closed to changing positions, to considering a differing viewpoint, and to learning new skills. Many with LSE choose, instead, to shut themselves off from new or opposing information and contradictory input because they don't trust their own ability to sort it out. In so doing, they resist change and cling to outdated beliefs for which they have no rationale other than familiarity. For example, people who've been raised in a family where education wasn't given much importance are less likely to do well in school or go on to college than families who place a high value on education. Or if someone comes from a poor and uneducated family, they may simply think that education is beyond their grasp and so rule it out as a possibility. Either way, they may not consider doing something different, they fail to consider other options.

Similarly, people born and raised in a particular religion may continue to think of themselves in conjunction with that religion whether or not they attend services. While calling themselves Baptists or Presbyterians, they may neither understand what their religion espouses nor live by its doctrine because religion to them represents traditions they are familiar with, rather than a belief system they have thoroughly examined and embraced. In the same way, those raised in Republican homes may not be able to say why they subscribe to that particular party or what the party stands for beyond one or two prominent issues. More importantly, they are not likely to figure out for themselves what they believe, but will, instead, conform to their narrow understanding of the party's goals. Thus they are followers, wanting to be told what's right, so that they don't have to make decisions, willing to let others dictate their beliefs.

What an LSE sufferer needs to do in recovery, however, is just the opposite. Because you have low self-esteem, which implies that your early environment was fraught with unhealthy behaviors and attitudes, you are strongly encouraged here to consistently question your beliefs and values and to decide, independently of your early influences, what you really believe and what you really think. You do not have to rely on or cling to the beliefs or attitudes of your family of origin; you can now make your own decisions. Part of the rights and privileges as an adult is that we each get to decide what we believe, what we value, what we cherish; we get to choose our own spiritual and political path, our own priorities, our own standards. You don't have to believe the negative and distorted information you may have received.

All too often, however, those with low self-esteem choose the path of least resistance, wanting to be spoon-fed out of fear of making a mistake, wanting others to make their decisions so they don't have to be responsible later on for their choices. In so doing, they also continue to accept destructive feedback and treatment by the dysfunctional family and community that originally shaped their low self-esteem.

Wally is desperate to be in a relationship or to at least have friends. Shy as a boy with a dominating mother and quiet father, Wally seldom observed his father communicating with other men or modeling behaviors about how to make and maintain friendships. Mostly Wally spent time with his brothers, where the relationship had been built by years of living together. Now Wally's brothers live far away and his father is no longer living, and Wally has had little success in developing relationships with either men or women. He is lonely, but he is also completely oblivious to the fact that he has low self-esteem—that he has problems—and doesn't even consider getting help. Though he is now 54 and has no friend he can call to do something with, he tells himself, "My brothers didn't need help to develop relationships. They both have great wives and friends. I just haven't had the same opportunities to meet the right people." So Wally continues his life, unwilling to do anything different, too embarrassed to admit he might need help.

> **NOTE:** *If we wish to develop healthy self-esteem, we must be willing to get help when we don't know what to do differently, be open to learning what we need to know, be willing to evaluate all information for its validity, be willing to examine ourselves when our efforts go unrewarded, and then to make our own informed decisions. As we do so, we will increase our confidence and our ability to make good choices. Putting off making decisions only makes us more fearful of doing so; making decisions whether good or bad and then learning from the process is what enables us to learn to make good choices and gives us control over our futures.*

2M-1. What beliefs do you hold only because they were first taught to you (i.e., you have never examined them? For instance, are you prejudiced toward others of a different race, different economic status, different sexual orientation for no reason other than that you were raised by people who were prejudiced of these groups of people? Do you hold certain political beliefs that you've never really looked at? Do you have views about marriage and child-rearing that you've never really thought through? Do you tend to think that people should all act, dress, and do things in a certain way?

_____

_____

_____

_____

_____

_____

_____

_____

_____

_____

2M-2. Think of two incidents where you rigidly held on to a belief that you didn't even fully understand until it hurt you or someone you cared about.

_____

_____

_____

_____

_____

_____

_____

2M-3. What do you think you could do to become more open to new ideas, new ways of looking at life and the people you encounter? For instance, could you read books, go to workshops on communication, join organizations where there is obvious diversity, listen to politicians who say they represent your party and examine whether you agree with their position rather than just taking it as the only point of view worth considering?

_____

_____

_____

_____

_____

_____

_____

_____

_____

➲   *Please go forward to **Obstacle 3, "Establishing the Source of Your LSE"** (page 256 in this book) and work through page 263. Instructions on page 263 will tell you where to go next.*

Obstacle 2, Excursion N

People with LSE are their own worst enemies

One of the consequences of low self-esteem is that those who have it become their own worst enemies. Their distorted thinking, their fear and anxiety, their inability to know who and when to trust, their anger and their pain, all lead them to do and say things that are not in their best interest. Or they fail to do or say things that would be to their benefit. A step toward recovery is acknowledging that, in all likelihood, we are acting in ways that are self-defeating and that we can alter the pattern. To do so, however, we must:

1. Be willing to face the fact that our own behaviors, primarily those of our conditioned thinking patterns, are sustaining and cementing our low self-esteem and are preventing us from being free to live our lives as we want. And because the end result is that we feel depressed, anxious, fearful, angry, etc., we must also realize that the way to alter these negative emotions is to work backwards in determining what we first said to ourselves that led us to feel so badly. We must remember that these emotions are generally only symptoms of a much deeper problem, i.e., low self-esteem, especially when these emotions are situational and result from our responses and reactions to those situations.

2. Become aware of our own distorted thoughts and then be willing to admit that they cause us to do and say—or fail to do and say—things that later cause us additional grief, thereby adding to our already low view of ourselves. Thus, not only do our negative self-statements keep us from doing the things we want to do, they further erode our view of self, making it highly unlikely we will ever be able to respond differently unless and until we get into recovery. We must be willing to take personal responsibility for each new area of awareness, working with determination to alter dysfunctional patterns and to dismantle our distorted thought patterns. Once we comprehend that it is our own self-talk that is maintaining our low self-esteem, we can no longer use our past as an excuse for what we do and do not know—or what we lack the courage to do. Once we are conscious of our problem, it is our responsibility and ours alone to find the solution and to make the necessary changes to live fulfilling lives. For this is what it means to be an adult—that we take responsibility for ourselves, our actions, our lives.

2N-1. Can you think of times in your life when you read into the behavior of others motivations or intentions that you later realized were inaccurate? Describe below three such incidents and what the consequences were.

1st incident:

_____

_____

_____

_____

2nd incident:

_____

_____

_____

_____

3rd incident:

_____

_____

_____

_____

REMEMBER: *You feel after you think. Mature behavior should be based on a combination of the two: thinking through the situation and the options and consequences, considering how you feel, and then drawing a conclusion. Some people only base their behavior on feelings, which gets them into trouble. They may spend money impulsively, for example, buying something just because they want it without considering that the Visa bill is due or that they don't have any extra money. Others may skip school or work because they don't feel like going. They don't consider the consequences but only live for the moment. Such immature people may not clean their houses, may not get the groceries, may not cook, or may not take care of their children because once again they don't feel like doing it, an attitude that makes them undependable and irresponsible. It's easy to see, therefore, that basing decisions on feelings alone can get us into trouble.*

Making decisions on the basis of feelings is also a huge problem for the individual with LSE because her feelings are based on irrational and distorted thinking. It's not the immature thinking of those described above, but it can look the same at times. The motivating factor, however, is fear: of rejection and disapproval, of proving her inadequacy, of affirming her incompetence. In both this case and those above, the core issue is one of inappropriate self-talk. The irresponsible person convinces himself that he has "a right to do what he wants to do and thinks he shouldn't have to do anything he doesn't want to do" and that "he deserves to do and get what he wants when he wants it." In the case of the person with LSE, he tells himself he isn't deserving or worthy, that he shouldn't expect too much, that the worst will probably happen, and that he had better protect himself. Both are examples of inaccurate and irrational thinking, and both cause grief and long-term negative consequences. Therefore, we have to regularly examine what we say to ourselves—our self-talk—for its validity until we become experts at recognizing our dysfunctional thinking patterns.

2N-2. Try to remember specifically what you said to yourself prior to each of the above incidents that led you to inaccurate conclusions or reactions. Write down at least three statements that you remember saying to yourself during each incident. For instance, did you say, "He's just using me—he really doesn't care" or "They only want me to come to the bowling party so they have someone to laugh at" or "I'm not going. I'd only make a fool out of myself"?

1st incident:

_____

_____

_____

_____

2nd incident:

_____

_____

_____

_____

3rd incident:

_____

_____

_____

_____

2N-3. One at a time, look closely at the statements in 2N-2 that you said to yourself and that led you to behave in the way you did. Ask yourself if each is true, factual, and based on history. In other words, if you've always been a good student but you talked yourself out of going to graduate school because you thought you couldn't do it, that statement is false based on your history of being a good student. Or if you tell yourself you're a bad driver because you were responsible for a fender bender after 22 years of driving without an accident, that accusation is just not factual. One accident in 22 years doesn't make anyone a bad driver. Now examine each of your assertions and note the inaccuracies.

1st incident:

_____

_____

_____

_____

2nd incident:

_____

_____

_____

_____

3rd incident:

_____

_____

_____

_____

2N-4. Now that you have located the statements that were irrational and not factual, what could you have said to yourself instead that would have been based on truth or fact? Write down a sentence that replaces the false statement, one that is based on truth, fact, or history to the extent that you know it. For example, "Maybe he likes me. I do like him. I guess I'll give him a chance" or "I think I'll go to the bowling party. I'm a pretty good bowler, and it'll give me a chance to get to know my coworkers better" or "It doesn't matter how good I am. We're really just going to be together and have a good time."

1st incident:

_____

_____

_____

_____

2nd incident:

_____

_____

_____

_____

3rd incident:

_____

_____

_____

_____

There is no way to appropriately emphasize the significance of the above exercise. This exercise represents the beginning of the removal of a major impediment in the journey to recovering from LSE: dismantling your negative and irrational self-talk. Our ability to complete it is the crux of overcoming Obstacle 2. The steps to doing so include:

1. Becoming aware of our self-talk and recognizing specific statements we make to ourselves following an incident

2. Analyzing those specific statements for truth, fact, and history

3. Learning to replace any negative, inaccurate statements with neutral or positive true assertions

4. Beginning a regimented program of repeating these statements over and over to ourselves until they become the basis of our thinking

2N-5. Can you think of times when you were overly sensitive and had your feelings hurt, but when, in fact, the other person really hadn't said or done anything wrong? Instead, you overreacted or misread the situation. Describe below three such incidents and what the consequences were.

1st incident:

_____

_____

_____

2nd incident:

_____

_____

_____

3rd incident:

_____

_____

_____

➲   *Before continuing, please read pages 254-262 of **Breaking the Chain of Low Self-Esteem**.*

*When you have finished reading those pages, please go forward to **Obstacle 4, "Catching Up"** (page 282 in this book) and work through page 283. Instructions on page 283 will tell you where to go next.*

Obstacle 2, Excursion O

Committing Ourselves to the Truth

LSE recovery requires that you look closely at your self-talk, analyzing it for its truthfulness and accuracy. In other words, if you have low self-esteem, you need to tell yourself on a regular basis that it is highly likely that your self-talk is distorted and inaccurate, not because you are a bad or dishonest person—but quite the opposite— because you believe you should not deceive yourself and set yourself up for disappointment or failure. For instance, you do not want to deceive yourself by thinking you will succeed at college, a new job, or some other challenge when you doubt you can do so. You don't want to set up expectations that you may meet someone wonderful, who will love and cherish you, when you feel unlovable. You don't want to push yourself to go to the party when you've already convinced you will have a miserable time and regret it later. You don't want to try to develop a new skill when you believe you will surely fail and be humiliated in the process.

The truth, however, is that most people who have low self-esteem are much more talented than they give themselves credit for. They have abilities they don't allow themselves to acknowledge; they are or could be likeable if they could only relax and become less self-absorbed. They are perfectly lovable and could develop the skills necessary to build good lives and solid, loving relationships, if they only pushed themselves to do so. Unfortunately, self-doubt, fear of failure, feelings of inadequacy, and beliefs that they are unworthy and unlovable can cripple or paralyze those with LSE, clouding their thinking, inhibiting their creativity, stifling their motivation, and preventing them from doing what is necessary to climb out of the dark hole of LSE. Instead, they maintain the vicious cycle of self-sabotage.

In the beginning, it is very difficult to see that our way of viewing ourselves and others is skewed; it is difficult to recognize that what we say to ourselves may not be accurate. In fact, we may need someone to help us see this, whether a therapist, a close friend, or a family member who is interested in our recovery and who has our best interests in mind. Having access to a support person on a regular basis is best, because as you go through recovery, this person will be able to point out irrational thinking that you may not be able to see but that you practice frequently. Since the goal is to closely examine each self-statement that pertains to a decision you make or a conclusion you draw for its accuracy based on history and evidence, don't hesitate to check out these thoughts with your support person so that you stay on track. Doing so will give you more confidence in making future decisions.

- **Continuing to analyze our self-talk**

    Along with the first principle of LSE recovery that you should memorize, *"feelings are the result of thinking,"* a second phrase that is equally helpful to remember is *"When my thinking is negative, it is most likely distorted and inaccurate due to my LSE."* Unfortunately, when it comes to trusting your analysis of yourself and your abilities as well as your analysis of others and their reactions to you, this is a universal consequence of LSE.

    As you continue to do the exercises in this book and then follow up using the ***Self-Esteem Recovery Toolkit,*** your distorted self-talk and self-defeating behavior will become more apparent. Being able to recognize and face your self-destructive behavior and the ways in which you program yourself for failure requires courage, but it will pay off in your recovery process. As you become more honest with yourself, you will gradually become more able to ascertain what is real and what is not, so that your actions will be based on fact and truth rather than on the distorted thinking that accompanies LSE. And, since your feelings are the result of your thinking, as your thinking becomes more rational and based on truth, so will your feelings. When this happens, your mood swings will level out, your episodes of depression and devastation will subside, your self-esteem attacks will become less frequent, and your overall experience of low self-esteem will lessen in intensity and in frequency.

- **Determining to base self-statements on truth**

    Hopefully, you are beginning to see how the way we talk to ourselves causes us to feel the way we do. Imagine for a minute that every time you were about to drive your car, you spent 15-30 minutes telling yourself all the horrible things that might happen. You might get in an accident—after all, your mind sometimes wanders; you might actually be the one to cause an accident—after all, on occasion you have been negligent or made a mistake. You might tell yourself that your car could have a tire blow out—since it's always a possibility. You might injure someone or you might get injured yourself—because you surely can't drive for everyone else on the road. Your car might malfunction—since you never know when that might happen. Or you might get a ticket—after all, you've made poor decisions before and gotten a ticket. You might say, "What if I get stranded alone somewhere? I wouldn't know what to do!" If you engaged in such self-talk each time you were about to drive your car, you would become fearful of driving and become overly anxious, and you would likely become a hazard on the road. Furthermore, you might quit driving altogether, because you would have repeatedly reinforced the idea that you were inadequate at driving. All these "what-if" statements suggest the *possibility* of something negative happening *if* you decide to engage in the activity in question. They are also the type of statements that comprise a major part of the self-talk of people with low self-esteem. As LSE sufferers have continued to tell themselves that they are inadequate, they have begun to doubt their ability to do many other things that most people routinely do. The person with low self-esteem fears he will confirm his own feelings of inadequacy and reveal it to others. Consequently, he becomes hyper-vigilant, trying to anticipate the potential pitfalls "if" he engages in a particular behavior and thereby increasing his anxiety. He questions every new activity, every new situation, every possible avenue of his life for elements that could be hazardous to his well-being. In essence, he "what-ifs" each possibility to death, saying "what-if *this*" or "what-if *that*"?

Sara's beach trip

Sara is asked by coworkers to join them on a weekend trip to the beach, about a two-hour drive from where they live. Immediately, her self-esteem issues are activated and she begins to question whether she should go. "What if I get over there and wish I hadn't gone? I won't be able to come back home. What if I do or say something out of line? After all, I don't know these women very well. What if they ask me to drive my car? I always get flustered when others are in the car. What if I have to share a room with one of the women I don't know? What would I say? What I should wear? What if I'm not dressed like they are? What if they suggest doing something I don't know how to do? What if they go off in little groups and ignore me? Or what if they want to go out in a boat? I'm afraid of water. What if I ask how much it's going to cost and I can't afford it? Then I'll really be embarrassed. What if I just don't fit in? What if they don't like me? What if they talk about things I don't know anything about? What if they ask why I don't have a boyfriend? What will I say?

What do you think is the likelihood that Sara will go on the beach trip? You're right; she won't. She will talk herself out of it by "what-if-ing" herself into such fear that she will make up an excuse of an engagement that she has forgotten.

What-ifs are simply suggestions of possible happenings. They could just as easily be positive, which is more the pattern of those with healthy self-esteem.

Lana and the beach trip

Lana is asked by coworkers to join them in a weekend trip to the beach, about a two-hour drive from where they live. She is immediately excited and tells herself that this will be an opportunity to get more acquainted with her coworkers. She begins thinking of other possible positive outcomes. What if she finds one woman in the group that she can become close pals with? Maybe she will find she really likes them all. Wouldn't that be great? She is confident that she can fit in and even thinks that she might learn some things from them, like where there are good places to eat, a good place to stay, and good shops. She thinks there are other possibilities as well: for instance, maybe they will go to some areas of the beach she hasn't been to before. That would be great. Maybe they will want to go deep-sea fishing. Wouldn't that be a cool adventure? Lana tells herself that the trip will be fun and begins talking to the women about the arrangements and what clothes to take.

What a difference self-talk makes. The results are astounding. One way is self-defeating, the other is uplifting; one discourages involvement in life and creates dread while the other raises spirits and anticipation. Both are the result of a preconceived self-view and the self-talk that accompanies it. Working backwards since we can't undo what is done, the LSE sufferer must focus on altering the self-talk that preprograms her to a life of avoidance and unhappiness.

"What ifs" are very dangerous and can completely distort the truth thereby affecting one's basis for decision making. For instance, in the scenario above about driving, one can say that she has been negligent or preoccupied at times or she can say that most of the time she is alert and attentive when she drives. She can focus on the one time she got a ticket or was in an accident, or she can remind herself of the 29 years she has driven with only one ticket or only one accident. It all depends where she puts the emphasis based on history. She also must be factual and be careful of generalizing—one accident or history is neither an indication that she is a bad driver nor a predictor of unpleasant things to come.

On this journey toward recovery three rules are very helpful. These include:

1. *deciding that you will only tell yourself the truth and that you will only act upon what you know to be true.*

2. *making a commitment to forming your own values and beliefs rather than adopting the beliefs of others without question.*

3. *deciding that you will not live your life on the basis of "what-ifs" but that, once again, you will only make decisions on the basis of truth, fact, and history.*

That means that you dedicate yourself to filtering out these self-statements that suggest negative possibilities, the self-talk that is discouraging without any basis of fact, and the assertions that are not based on what has been true for you in the past.

2O-1. On the lines below, describe three incidents in which your actions were controlled by "what-ifs"—times when you either did or failed to do something because you talked yourself out of it using "What-if" self-statements. For instance, did you stay home from an outing you would like to have attended because you said to yourself, "What if I don't know anyone there" or "What if a particular person that I don't like is there"?

1st incident:

_____
_____
_____
_____

2nd incident:

_____
_____
_____
_____

3rd incident:

_____
_____
_____
_____

2O-2. How did you feel after you allowed your "what-ifs" to dictate your response? Did you wish later that you had taken a chance? Did you realize that you had talked yourself out of doing something for no valid reason?

1st incident:

_____
_____
_____
_____

2nd incident:

_____

_____

_____

_____

3rd incident:

_____

_____

_____

_____

Make a commitment today that you will not allow your life to be controlled or affected by "What-ifs," that you will only base your actions and decisions on what you know to be true.

➲   *Please go forward to **Obstacle 4, "Catching Up"** (page 284 in this book) and work through page 285. Instructions on page 285 will tell you where to go next.*

OBSTACLE 3

Establishing the Source of Your LSE

To begin to recognize that your personal tapes are indeed distorted and how this has happened, to see that they are now negatively influencing, even negatively destroying, your life, you must thoroughly examine your background. This means looking back at your family of origin and the ways in which your family members and other significant people in your life are intertwined with the specific circumstances and events of your life. Coming to understand what has led you to view yourself so negatively is absolutely essential to fully understanding how your tape became inaccurate. Until you can grasp the specific incidents, behaviors, and attitudes that led to your distorted self-view, full recovery cannot occur.

One aspect of low self-esteem is frequently misunderstood: the timetable of when and how a person develops it. You have probably heard someone say that following a particularly difficult time or circumstance, she developed low self-esteem, e.g., after a job loss, as the result of an abusive relationship, or following some other particularly devastating situation. Without fully understanding exactly what low self-esteem is and how deep-seated it is, this idea seems feasible; it is, however, inaccurate.

Low self-esteem is entirely a thinking problem. In other words, LSE is a consistent, negative pattern of thinking that is based on an all-encompassing view of an inadequate self. This is not to say that the person with low self-esteem thinks she is without skills or is totally lacking in redeeming qualities, nor that she is at all times conscious of the fear and anxiety that accompanies her LSE. Rather, at some level, whether buried or accessible, she believes she is less deserving, less adequate, less able, or less competent than "regular" people in being able to cope and succeed in all aspects of her life. Her negative view of herself, may NOT be apparent to others, nor is she necessarily aware that she views herself differently than others view themselves. In fact, her LSE may only surface in specific situations when these self-doubts are stirred up. In other words, she may feel very confident in her ability to do her present work, where expectations are clear and her ability has been proven. However, she will experience her LSE when she is offered a promotion or asked to address others at a departmental meeting. Or she may feel her self-doubts and feelings of inadequacy surface in new social situations, when she is engaged in unfamiliar activities or when she is evaluating the affection and integrity of someone she cares about. The point is that this pattern of thinking of the self as inadequate has been with her since childhood, no matter how latent it is or how seldom experienced. When as an adult, she is challenged to do something she feels unprepared to do, or when she is in a relationship that is moving toward intimacy, the irrational fear and anxiety that has lain dormant crops up, her negative self-talk is reactivated, and she instantly feels confused and incapable of dealing with the situation at hand.

This problem is quite different for a person who has felt capable and acceptable for years but who, due to a specific negative circumstance or a situational tragedy or crisis, has temporarily become disillusioned or depressed. When the crisis passes, this person, who has always enjoyed healthy self-esteem will gradually regain her motivation and direction; this is normal. Her years of coping, achieving, and believing in herself will help her to rebound and regain her stability. On the other hand, the person with low self-esteem has never known what it feels like to fully accept himself; he does not have that experience to draw upon. Instead, he has always "known," somewhere deep within himself, that he is not like other people, that something is indeed lacking within him. Accordingly, he has spent a lifetime trying to camouflage his weaknesses, hide his inadequacies, and avoid circumstances where his flaws might be visible to others. He feels abnormal at times and experiences an uneasy but unidentifiable apprehension of danger. He feels lacking in basic life skills but doesn't know what they are and is too embarrassed to ask for help; he is fearful of doing something inappropriate and humiliating himself.

Many people who come to therapy because of self-esteem issues are wholly aware of how their low self-esteem was formed. Having long analyzed their childhoods, they can quickly point out the culprits who destroyed their self-esteem: their parents or other individuals, plus a wide variety of circumstances that singly or together formed a dysfunctional developmental environment. In this environment, they were overly criticized, berated, neglected, and physically, emotionally, or sexually abused; they felt unloved, discouraged, frustrated, angry, demeaned, unsupported, over-disciplined, etc. Some grew up in homes where alcohol-dependent or drug-dependent family members abused them, abused a fellow family member, or abused one another; others come from families where parents were emotionally unhealthy, bitter, or unstable. That these home situations do not lend themselves to the development of healthy children goes without saying, but exactly how these aspects affect a child's self-esteem has not been fully understood. While hundreds of books have been written on the results of abuse, most people, including most professionals, have not understood how—or the extent to which—low self-esteem destructively affects a person's thinking and behavior, nor have they understood that LSE begins in childhood, not as the result of a singular adult event.

Deciding to seek therapy is a difficult decision for those with low self-esteem because it means they will have to reveal their most private feelings and thoughts, something they may never have done before. Believing they are uniquely dysfunctional, this thought of sharing in depth with another person, especially one whose job it is to analyze them, is very frightening. And all too often they go to therapy totally unaware that they have low self-esteem, only to be misdiagnosed so that the therapy is ineffective. (For more information on how low self-esteem is ignored and misdiagnosed, read Dr. Sorensen's second book, *Low Self-Esteem: Misunderstood & Misdiagnosed,* Wolf Publishing Co., 2001)

So the first battle to be won by the person with low self-esteem is to become fully conscious of the fact that you have low self-esteem and that LSE is a valid—and serious—mental health problem in and of itself *and one that is treatable.* The second step is two-fold: first beginning to understand the dysfunctional behavior patterns that accompany your LSE so that they can be altered, and second, starting to sort through your background, like a detective painstakingly attempting to solve a crime, until gradually the evidence begins to surface and you start to comprehend how your problem first developed. Until you can comprehend that your LSE was neither *caused by you nor deserved by you,* you will not be equipped to correct the problem.

Many people who enter therapy go to great lengths to defend their parents and their backgrounds as typical and ordinary. Claiming that they enjoyed a satisfying and normal childhood, these clients are extremely reluctant to point the finger at parents or anyone close to them who might possibly have contributed to their LSE. In every case, and over time, however, as the person relates and listens to his stories about his childhood and receives feedback about the inappropriateness of some of the behaviors towards him, this changes. Gradually, he begins to recognize the dysfunctional patterns that existed and which served as a foundation for the irrational and distorted self-view that has so damaged his life, and he begins to feel anger and a deep sadness.

It is impossible to express the significance of this recognition of the origin of your low self-esteem to your success in overcoming this problem. Please understand that it is absolutely critical that you do so, *for until you are able to acknowledge that your negative view of self began as the result of inappropriate and unhealthy behaviors and attitudes on the part of others,* you cannot begin to question the validity of the messages you received, digested, and accepted as truth—messages that now so destructively influence your life.

And if you are someone who has not been able to determine the source of your low self-esteem, don't worry; many people need time to accurately recollect the past, to reflect on those recollections, and to become clear about how these memories fit together before they can accurately assess responsibility. Early and consistent messages to "honor, respect, and obey" our parents have created in many of us a reticence to analyze, criticize, or view them as real people with their own flaws and limitations, people who were also the product of their own early (and quite often dysfunctional) environments. Acceptance of our belief in our own shortcomings has cemented the belief that we and we alone are to blame for our inadequacies, rather than others who were instrumental in shaping our understanding of ourselves.

For most LSE sufferers, this will be a topic to revisit throughout your recovery process. Whether or not you recognize how and where your low self-esteem developed, there is an additional step that you must take: realizing why the messages received from this dysfunctional environment are, in fact, distorted. This important aspect is discussed more fully later in this section.

Obstacle 3 is "Establishing the Source of Your LSE," a journey into examining the past, through a number of excursions—smaller treks into the hills and valleys of the past. Ii is strongly suggested that you read through the material in each of these treks and respond to the questions, even if you are certain that you know how your low self-esteem evolved. Some of the exercises may seem simplistic and insignificant, but each serves a purpose, laying the groundwork for ultimately changing a distorted view of yourself to one that is accurate, truthful, and factual. I recommend that you do not try to evaluate the outcome of each journey: just plunge in and work your way through them. Over time your progress will become apparent.

Obstacle 3, Excursion A

What we know and learn as babies and toddlers

Babies do not have skills when they are born. While they cry when hungry or in pain and may react to loud noises, they haven't formed opinions, they haven't obtained knowledge, they haven't acquired skills. Immediately following birth, however, they begin to assess their environment and develop an outlook on the world and how they fit into it, gradually learning who and when to trust, gradually learning the rules they must live by to survive. It's commonly understood that the most critical years of our development are the first five: it is in these early months and years that we develop a view of self, a perspective that solidifies during these early years and stays with us until some specific intervention alters it.

3A-1. List 5 skills that you think are among the first ones that a baby develops. (For instance, they are able to hear and focus on where sound is coming from, they are also able to respond by cooing or making small noises, they are able to show their discomfort by crying.)

1._____

2._____

3._____

4._____

5._____

3A-2. Do you have any reason to believe that the skills you learned as a baby were any different from these? If so place an X before the skill(s) above you think you may not have learned as a baby and explain on the lines below why you believe this to be true.

_____

_____

_____

_____

_____

NOTE: *Your comments above and below are important because they may indicate that you had a physical problem at a very early age that might account for:*

- *why your parents were overly protective, possible giving you the impression that you were inadequate*
- *why your early months or years were unusual (many doctors appointments, ongoing surgeries)*
- *why one or both parents felt it necessary to work extra jobs and be gone from home more, leading you to later feel abandoned or unloved*
- *why your care-taking involved additional family members, nurses, etc., so that you didn't bond well with your primary parent*

3A-3. What factors do you think affect how—and when—babies develop the skills you listed in 3A-1 (for example does a baby need attention and external stimulation)?

_____

_____

_____

_____

_____

_____

3A-4. List 5 things that you think are among the first pieces of information a baby hears and learns (for example, loud voices, sharp tones of voice, and what they indicate, mothers voice).

1._____

2._____

3._____

4._____

5._____

3A-5. Do you have any reason to believe that the information you acquired as a baby was any different from this? If so, place an X before the item(s) above that you think you may not have learned as a baby and explain below why you think this is true.

_____

_____

_____

_____

_____

_____

3A-6. What factors do you think affect how—and when—babies learn what they learn?

_____

_____

_____

_____

_____

_____

3A-7. Explain any other information you have that might explain how your first weeks and months of life were abnormal or influenced by unusual circumstances. (For example, did your mother die at childbirth? Was either parent seriously ill or away at war at the time? Were you a twin? Was your family living in poverty? Was either parent blind, deaf, or otherwise disabled?)

_____

_____

_____

_____

_____

_____

3A-8. List 5 skills that you think are among those a toddler develops. (For instance, they learn to crawl, to stand, to put words together.)

1._____

2._____

3._____

4._____

5._____

3A-9. Do you have any reason to believe that the skills you learned as a toddler were any different from these? If so place an X before the skill(s) above you think you may not have learned as a toddler and explain on the lines below why you believe this to be true.

_____

_____

_____

_____

_____

_____

3A-10. What factors do you think affect how—and when—toddlers develop the skills you listed in 3-A.8? (For example, does having an older sibling affect how early a child begins to talk?)

_____

_____

_____

_____

_____

_____

3A-11. List 5 things that you think are among the first pieces of information a toddler learns.

1._____

2._____

3._____

4._____

5._____

3A-12. Explain any other information you have that might explain how your early years of life were abnormal or influenced by unusual circumstances.

_____

_____

_____

_____

_____

_____

_____

_____

NOTE: *Do not be upset or tell yourself negative things if you are unable to remember specifics about the questions above. Most people do not remember these things but have been told stories by their parents or older siblings that enable them to reflect on and discuss these factors. Most people will not have anything unusual to report, but for those who do, these details may have been significant to the development of their low self-esteem.*

Recap of "What we know and learn as babies and toddlers": *After rereading your responses to Excursion A, can you see anything unusual in your first years of life that might have contributed to the development of your low self-esteem? If so summarize and explain here:*

_____

_____

_____

_____

_____

_____

_____

_____

_____

_____

➲   *Please go back to **Obstacle 2, "Rewriting the Script"** (page 35 in this book) and work through page 44. Instructions on page 44 will tell you where to go next.*

Obstacle 3, Excursion B

The Positive Things I Remember Thinking About Myself

Many people are unable to remember facts about their early lives or how they felt about themselves or saw themselves as children, preadolescents, and teenagers, while others are able to relate stories; to describe numerous incidents, even minute details; and to recall specific conversations from their early years and how they felt about themselves and their surroundings. There are generally specific reasons why people can't remember the past; for instance, many have simply blocked out what was too painful to remember. However, this problem can usually be circumvented as the desire to remember gradually becomes greater than the fear these memories invoke. Either way, be patient with yourself, going through each exercise and responding as best you can. Allow yourself to pass over the questions you have no response to and then plan to revisit them later. The ability to recall information from your past and then digest it is a process that will happen over time anyway; there is no urgency to remember your entire childhood and youth at this moment, so there is no need to make yourself overly anxious that you cannot remember more. A trick to remembering, however, is to try first to imagine the home you lived in at any particular point in your life, picturing each room as you can and then activities that went on in that room. Try to remember whose bedroom was whose and how it looked. Try to picture the kitchen and family meals. Try to think about what the family did after dinner and in which room, and who came and went from the home. Think about significant events like the birth of a sibling or an illness or accident a member of the family had. Then try to picture the outside of your home and what you did there, gradually moving from home to school and so on. Sometimes focusing first on the backdrop is less threatening and thus an easier place to begin than trying to remember the actors and their parts in the scenario.

As you move through this workbook, you will encounter exercises that are specifically intended to help stimulate your memories. Relax. Relax. Relax. Don't push yourself too hard. As you contemplate these questions over time and begin to understand the value of remembering rather than just the pain they conjure up, memories will begin to surface.

This entire experience deals with both general and specific memories. As you move through your journey of overcoming Obstacle 3, you will find the questions becoming more specific and possibly more relevant as we address the significant people in your life. For instance, one entire set of inquiries will be devoted to your relationship with your mother and another to your relationship with your father, so there is some unavoidable overlap. Do not feel as though you have to say everything you can remember in this section at this time. You can always go back and add more if you wish, and later sections may well address the issue in more detail.

3B-1. List 4 POSITIVE things you remember *thinking* and *believing* about yourself. Behind each positive thought or belief you list, choose 2 words from the Feelings List that describe how it felt to think or believe this about yourself. (For example: as a teenager, Janet remembers thinking that she was smart and a good student, that she was very athletic, that she was good at math, and that she was a nice person who cared about others. As a result she felt: ambitious and motivated, capable and energized, encouraged and hopeful, understood and appreciated.)

- As a young child (Janet remembers thinking of herself as obedient, respectful, sensitive, and helpful.)

1. Funny _____ Ed told me
   Wrote good rhyming poems. _____ 5th grade teacher
2. _____ read 1 in class.

_____

3. _____

_____

4. _____

_____

- As a preadolescent   Compared myself favorably to pics of ♀ in mags
                         who Did their appearance & make up;
1. Nice face,   I didn't think I needed any △.
   funny   Ed told me.
2. good speller   got into a spelling bee
   wrote clever rhyming lyrics   knew they were
3. to known songs   good at the time. (science
                       project.)
4. _____

_____

other girls were ?y their color. I didn't get this as mine was fine as it was.

- As a teenager

1. *Liked my natural haircolor* _____

_____

2. _____

_____

3. _____

_____

4. _____

_____

3B-2. Where did you get this information about your positive qualities? Go back to 3B-1 and next to each positive thought or belief you just listed, write down where you think this thought or belief originated. For instance, if you said, I'm a pretty good basketball player, was it because your father told you so? Then write, "My Dad told me so."

■

NOTE: *At this point, it is important to remind yourself that "feelings are the result of thinking," and that this applies as well to when you were young. Because you now have LSE, we know that sometime after birth, your thinking began to be distorted by some form of dysfunction within your environment; this resulted in the beginning of negative thoughts that then produced negative feelings about yourself.*

Consequently as a part of figuring out the source of your low self-esteem, you are being asked to describe what you remember thinking about yourself. This will enable you to eventually realize why you felt the things you did about yourself at that time. Here are some examples:

- *"I'm a fast runner" (my physical education teacher told the whole class that I'm the fastest).*
- *"I'm ugly" (my brother tells me so).*
- *"I'm a really bad kid" (Dad hit me last night).*
- *"Mom doesn't like me very well" (she criticizes me a lot), or "Mom wishes she had never had me" (Mom's often depressed and unavailable).*
- *"Dad likes my brother better than me" (he didn't punish my brother for not finishing his chores like he did me last night).*
- *"I never do anything right" (Mom is always telling me what I did wrong).*

■

Thus, first *we hear* direct feedback or comments made about us to others, or *we observe* someone's behavior toward us or toward someone else. Second, *we interpret* what we've seen and heard. Then, based on our interpretation of what we've seen, what we have heard, and *what we think we understand, we draw conclusions about what* is true and factual. From then on, we use these conclusions as the basis for the way we view ourselves and others and as the basis for the way we talk to ourselves *about* ourselves and others. Sometimes our interpretations *are factual and based on the truth;* other times they are not. Sometimes what we have seen and been told is *based on fact;* other times it is not. Instead, it is merely the inaccurate or distorted interpretation of others. As we get older and if we have been taught truth and fact, we are better able to discern fact from distortions. Children, however, have little or no basis of comparison, experience, or resources to draw upon in order to sort out what is truth and what is not, so they are easily influenced into believing what they hear or think they hear. Innocently, without question, and because their scope is so limited, they tell themselves that what is happening around them is about them and that what is being said to them is accurate; then their feelings correspond with this conclusion. Once a distorted perspective is formed, all other thinking and decision-making becomes based on this inaccurate conclusion.

This is especially true when the person giving the message (whether verbal or behavioral) is someone we consider significant, such as a parent, teacher, highly respected member of the community, respected uncle or grandparent, admired friend, etc. The more important we view the person to our lives, the more likely we are to believe that person's comments and to feel deserving of any reward or punishment that comes from them. And once this viewpoint about ourselves has been accepted and repeated in our thinking, our feelings coincide. Thus if we talk negatively to ourselves, whether or not these statements are based on truth, they become the creed by which we live.

Again, this very important principle, that feelings are the result of thinking is the foundation upon which low self-esteem is built and maintained; once you understand this premise, memorize it and repeat if to yourself often.

3B-3. If you have difficulty recognizing how your low self-esteem formed, it may be helpful to look at who the people were who had the most profound positive influence in your early life. Maybe, for instance, you will realize that there was no one who had a very positive affect on your early life or maybe you will realize that the most positive influences were outside your family of origin, helping you realize how negative your home environment really was. Name those who were *positive* influences and explain why you think of them this way. Then select one word from the Feelings List that describes how you felt about yourself when you were around that person. Write these down.

- As a child

1._____

_____

2._____

_____

3._____

_____

- As a preadolescent

1._____

_____

2._____

_____

3._____

_____

4._____

_____

- As a teenager

1._____

_____

2._____

_____

3._____

_____

4._____

_____

3B-4. Describe up to 4 of the most memorable and significant incidents that happened in any period of your youth that you now believe led you to think you might possess the positive qualities you listed in 3B-1, and name the two people who were of greatest influence overall in helping you believe this about yourself.

1._____

_____

2._____

_____

3._____

_____

4._____

_____

3B-5. Describe up to 4 of the most memorable and significant incidents that happened after you became an adult that led you to think you still had these or other positive qualities. Name the people whose words or actions were of the greatest influence overall in helping you believe this about yourself.

1._____

_____

2._____

_____

3._____

_____

4._____

_____

3B-6. Choose 3 feelings from the Feelings List that best describe how it felt in your youth to believe you possessed these positive qualities. Feel free to use your own words or phrases.

1._____

2._____

3._____

3B-7. Do you still believe you have these positive qualities? If not, explain why you don't think so. For instance, were there specific incidents that caused you to change your perspective about yourself in a specific area? If so, describe these incidents and how they affected your thoughts and beliefs about yourself.

_____

_____

_____

_____

_____

_____

_____

_____

Those who suffer from low self-esteem struggle with the competing and conflicting views they have of themselves. For instance, they may view themselves in many ways as bright, competent, and resourceful, yet when a situation arises that feels threatening, they are immediately reduced to feeling unable to cope or feeling totally incompetent to handle the situation. Thus, most people with low self-esteem feel quite capable and competent in many areas of their lives but have lingering self-doubts about their abilities in other parts of their existence. They may spend two years at a job where they are excelling at their work, then when unexpectedly asked to perform a task that they don't understand, they immediately become consumed with extreme and debilitating anxiety, feeling totally incompetent and fearful of failure and rejection. Thinking they "should" know how to perform the requested task, they are too humiliated to ask for assistance or admit that they haven't yet learned this skill. While those with high self-esteem would not think that competence requires knowing all there is to know about any one subject, those with LSE tend to have black-and-white thinking, they think that not knowing something, any one thing, implies incompetence, making them less valuable and dispensable. They can acquire extensive knowledge and perfect their skills but still feel all that is invalidated by one undeveloped skill, one unknown fact, or one mistake.

Recap of "The positive things I remember thinking about myself": *After rereading your responses to Excursion 3B write down any memories or thoughts about the basis for the development of your low self-esteem that have been sparked. If so, record your thoughts and memories here.*

_____

_____

_____

_____

_____

_____

_____

_____

_____

_____

_____

_____

_____

➲   *Please go back to **Obstacle 2, "Rewriting the Script"** (page 45 in this book) and work through page 51. Instructions on page 51 will tell you where to go next.*

Obstacle 3, Excursion C

The Negative Things I Remember Thinking About Myself

Even more important than recognizing who the positive influences in your life were and what the positive things you thought about yourself *were is being able to identify who the negative influences were in your life and what those individuals taught you about yourself.* Remember that there is no such thing as a "bad" child but merely one who needs guidance and appropriate discipline; that there is no such thing as an incompetent child but one who needs to be taught and encouraged; that there is no such thing as an unlovable child but one who needs to be loved, Thus if a child is misbehaving, there is some provocation; if a child hates himself, there are definite and destructive reasons.

3C-1. List 4 NEGATIVE things you remember thinking and believing about yourself. Then, behind each negative thought or belief that you list, choose 2 words from the Feelings List that describe how you felt thinking and believing this about yourself.

- As a child

1._____

_____

2._____

_____

3._____

_____

4._____

_____

- As a preadolescent

1._____

_____

2._____

3._____

4._____

- As a teenager

1._____

2._____

3._____

4._____

3C-2. Where did you get this information about your negative qualities? Go back to the negative thoughts or beliefs you just listed, and behind each negative thought or belief you had about yourself, write the reason for each thought or belief. For instance, if you said, "I'll never succeed in life," you might write, "My Dad told me I could never do anything right" or if you said that you thought you would never be able to achieve in school, it was because your sister had told you that you were dumb.

3C-3. Describe 4 situations that led you to think negatively about yourself. From the Feelings List, choose 3 words that best describe how you felt in each of these instances and place them next to the descriptions.

1._____

2._____

3._____

_____

_____

4._____

_____

_____

3C-4. Name the people or describe the incidents (and the people connected to those incidents) that you now believe had the most negative influence in your life and explain why you think this is true.

- As a child

1._____

_____

_____

_____

2._____

_____

_____

_____

3._____

_____

_____

_____

4._____

_____

_____

_____

- As a preadolescent

1._____

_____

_____

_____

2._____

_____

_____

3._____

_____

_____

_____

4._____

_____

_____

_____

- As a teenager

1._____

_____

_____

_____

2._____

_____

_____

_____

3._____

_____

_____

_____

4._____

_____

_____

_____

3C-5. Are any of these people still in your life today? If so, what type of relationship
do you have with each person now? Have you confronted any of them about the
way they treated you? Have they ever apologized or admitted to the ways in which
they wronged you as a child, preadolescent, or teenager?

_____

_____

_____

_____

_____

_____

_____

_____

_____

_____

_____

_____

_____

NOTE: *Children learn from what they see and hear. If a parent or other significant
adult is bitter about the circumstances of his own life and then releases his feelings onto
a child through degrading, demanding, or impatient remarks, that child will feel that she
is the cause of the adult's unhappiness. If a parent is emotionally or physically unavailable, the child will feel abandoned, unworthy, and unloved. If an unhealthy adult mistreats—or allows others—to mistreat a child, the child will feel that there is something
wrong with him, not the adult. Thus, the messages a child gets growing up may have
little to do with the child but may be a projection of the emotional instability or imma-
turity of the people in his life.*

*If a child's life is filled with negative influences; if that child lacks sufficient love,
support, guidance, encouragement, appropriate discipline, structure, is that child really*

responsible for lack of follow-through, for lack of ambition, or for inappropriate behavior? If a child grows up in an otherwise normal environment but has a mother who frequently degrades him, criticizes him, or embarrasses him in front of others, how can the child be expected to cope without becoming depressed or angry and then acting out? How can a child be expected to achieve without support, believe in herself without affirmation, or to face life's challenges without hope? Children do not spring from the womb motivated, ambitious, polite, or knowledgeable, nor are they born sullen, passive, or fearful. It is only with the appropriate guidance, unconditional love, and care that a child finds the right path to becoming a healthy adult. Certainly other influences enter into the child's life as she attends school and gets out into the community so that she is exposed to the rules of society and gets glimpses of what is and isn't appropriate behavior in a variety of situations. Yet, until the child develops the ability to reason and to understand these codes of behavior and until he develops self control, he may vent his anger inappropriately, he may be uncooperative and sullen, or he may be reclusive and depressed, all of which are self-defeating and affect his start in life. These are the possible ramifications of low self-esteem; these are the possible results for the child who develops a negative view of himself.

Up until now, you may have assumed that the negative things you were told about yourself were true. If so, it is time to consider otherwise—time to realize that we are all products of our environments and that these things you were told about yourself were likely untrue and the result of impatient, unskilled, uncommunicative, or emotionally unstable adults. Your negative view of yourself may then have been reinforced as you responded to the neglect or the abuse. For instance, you may have been told repeatedly that you were naughty as a child because you reacted to being ignored by doing things to try to get the attention you craved. If that is the situation you grew up in, you were not at fault and you were not a bad kid. If you acted out in anger as a result of being abused, you were not a bad kid either, only a confused and wounded one.

Children do not deserve unkind words that label them as bad, nor are they capable of separating truth from fiction. However, they are effective at internalizing negative attitudes and actions expressed toward them and then of acting out their feelings (remember: feelings are the result of thinking).

Consequently, if young children are neglected, treated harshly, ridiculed, overly criticized, or constantly provoked, they become the product of unhealthy people within a sickly environment, and the child's behavior reflects her anger, her discouragement, or her need for attention. As a child, she is not mature enough to sort out why these people treat her this way or how she should handle her emotions differently—she only acts upon her needs. If as she gets older, her behavior becomes more inappropriate, society will, of course, hold her responsible, and children who have had little or no guidance will be punished for the sins of the adults who raised them and interacted with them, so that the child remains a victim of her early environment at least until she goes through a program of recovery, thus, the importance of these exercises.

■

3C-6. Describe any attempts you have made to speak up, to make your feelings known, or to confront any of the people who had a negative influence on you.

- If you did any of these things, did you feel heard? Did you feel your confrontation was effective? If so, describe the positive results you think you achieved.

_____

_____

_____

_____

_____

_____

_____

- On the other hand, did you feel rebuffed, ignored, or dismissed when you tried to make your feelings known? Did anyone try to place the responsibility back on you or make you feel guilty for complaining? Explain.

_____

_____

_____

_____

_____

_____

_____

> **NOTE:** *Confrontation is very difficult for people who feel insecure or unsure of themselves. Feeling that they may deserve the ways others treat them, especially if the treatment is at the hands of authority figures, those who are mistreated often just swallow their feelings, thus avoiding the possibility of more negative feedback if they were to speak up and*
>
> *cont.*

> *voice their displeasure. Even the thought of confronting a person whose behavior seems obviously inappropriate elicits more fear of reprisal.*
>
> *Also, the complaints of young people against adults often go unheard or are invalidated by people who are naïve, uncaring, or too fearful themselves to seriously consider the ramifications and take the appropriate action. Young people who've made accusations that have been ignored know full well the embarrassment and pain of having their feelings dismissed as fantasy or exaggerations.*
>
> *Finally, it should be understood that confronting others is an act of assertiveness that even many adults do not practice and that becoming an assertive person requires the development of communication skills and confidence in oneself.*

3C-7.   Do you believe you still have these negative qualities you listed in 3C-1? Or that you ever had them? If so, list your reasons here. If not, how were you able to change them or what enabled you to see you never had them?

_____

_____

_____

_____

_____

_____

_____

_____

3C-8. If you answered yes to the last question, do you now see how the negative comments from others and behaviors of others were largely responsible for how you have viewed yourself over the years? Write down your thoughts.

_____

_____

_____

_____

_____

_____

3C-9. As a child, preadolescent, and teenager, you probably compared yourself to others. If so, how did you rate yourself? Check all that apply:
I felt:

	Child	Preadolescent	Teenager
• Less intelligent than others my age			
• More intelligent than others my age			
• Inferior in abilities to others my age	✓		
• Superior in abilities to others my age			
• Equal in abilities to others my age			
• Less popular than others my age	✓	✓	✓
• More popular than others my age			
• Less focused on pleasing people than others			
• More focused on pleasing people than others			
• Needing less attention than others			
• Needing more attention than others			
• Happier than others			
• Sadder than others	✓	✓	✓
• Angrier or more defiant than others		✓	✓
• More confused than others			
• More shy or frightened than others	✓	✓	✓
• More confident than others			
• Less confident than others	✓	✓	✓
• Having as many friends as others			
• Having fewer friends than others	✓	✓	✓
• Fitting in as well as others			
• Fitting in less well than others	✓	✓	✓
• In trouble more than others			
• More athletic than others			
• Less athletic than others	✓	✓	✓
• More attractive than others			

- Less attractive than others   _____   _____   _____
- More motivated than others   _____   _____   _____
- Less motivated than others   _____   _____   _____
- Treated by teachers as well as others   _____   _____   _____
- Not treated as well by teachers as others   _____   _____   _____

3C-10. Based on the blanks you filled in above, do you think you were emotionally needy? In other words, do you think you had more emotional needs than others your age? Explain.

- As a child

_____

_____

_____

- As a preadolescent

_____

_____

_____

- As a teenager

_____

_____

_____

Recap of "The negative things I remember thinking about myself":
After reconsidering your responses to this section:
- Are you now or have you previously been aware of anything negative you thought about yourself as a child or that you did as a child that directly stemmed from how you were treated or what you were told about yourself and that you understand contributed to the development of your low self-esteem? (For instance, did you think of yourself as inadequate or did you often strike out in anger?) If so, describe what you now realize about your thoughts or behavior:

_____

_____

_____

_____

_____

_____

_____

_____

_____

_____

_____

NOTE: *If you have listed being angry and striking out in anger,* be aware that *anger is an appropriate response to being mistreated you or to realizing that someone was responsible for the development of your low self-esteem. In fact, being able to be angry with the person or people who contributed to your LSE is a positive step toward recovery. Until you can point the finger at the true perpetrator, you are likely pointing it at yourself and blaming yourself for something that was clearly not your responsibility.*

People feel uncomfortable with this concept because it may mean being angry at their parents and they've been told to respect their parents. Remember, however, that your parents are only people; they have faults and they may have made critical mistakes in raising you. Being angry with them doesn't mean that you will automatically cease to love them, but it will mean placing guilt where it belongs and removing it from your shoulders. In fact, experiencing this anger is a necessary part of the process of recovery, enabling you to move along in realizing that you are not to blame for having developed LSE and that there is nothing basically wrong with you. Yes, you may lack skills, experience, and information—but you are not damaged beyond repair. Recovery is always an option and skills can still be learned.

➲   *Please go forward to* **Obstacle 4, "Catching Up"** *(page 269 in this book) and work through page 273. Instructions on page 273 will tell you where to go next.*

Obstacle 3, Excursion D

The Impact and Behavior of My Siblings

The actions, habits, interests, skills, and behaviors of each family member have a profound effect on every person in the family, whether the original family or a step-family. First, other family members are the primary source of feedback for most of us, especially at an early age, and secondly, because the lives of family members are so interwoven that the problems, responsibilities, and schedules of each member affect the lives of all the others. For instance, if one member of the family has a serious and lengthy illness or recovery from an accident, parents may unwittingly neglect other family members because they are tired and emotionally taxed. If one family member is addicted to drugs or alcohol, his problem can interfere with the family's plans and activities, create family disputes and financial problems, and cause embarrassment to parents, spouse, siblings, or children. His behaviors can also have an effect on how other people view and treat the rest of the family. If one member of the family is an outstanding athlete or scholar, expectations of the whole family and its standing in the society may increase. Conversely, if one sibling is a poor student or is often in trouble at school or with the law, teachers may expect less from other siblings and give them less attention, and parents may lose standing in the community.

In recovering from low self-esteem, it is important to reflect on the family constellation into which you were born. With time, distance, and maturity, you may now be able to see the past more clearly and to recognize events and people that more negatively influenced you than was obvious to you at a younger age. This is not a time to make excuses for the people in your life or to rationalize their behavior. Just as you are now accountable for becoming healthy and for responding appropriately to the people in your life, whether they be coworkers, spouse, children, or neighbors, so too the significant people in your life were responsible, regardless of their upbringing, for learning how to treat you and others appropriately. Remember that being dysfunctional, *and recognizing that you are,* is nothing to be ashamed of; however, choosing to remain dysfunctional once you realize it, is a choice.

Also, remember that no incident is trivial. If years later, you still remember a situation and feel bad about it, it was obviously significant; it made a strong enough impression on you at the time that it remains in your memory bank. Also, understand that an incident can be devastating to one person (because it is a reminder of abuse or negativity once experienced) and yet be less hurtful to another person who has not had to endure it repeatedly or who does not find it symbolic of a larger pattern of dysfunctional or inappropriate behavior. Thus, the fact that a particular situation might not be painful to someone else does not mean that it shouldn't be excruciating for you. *Furthermore, realize that the seed of doubt about our self-worth originates with one suggestion, one traumatic incident, one "put-down," one criticism.* If this or similar offenses occur in an environment that continues to be demeaning, unloving, and hurtful, our negative view of self becomes firmly implanted.

If you have already examined your relationship during your youth to other family members and think you thoroughly understand the dynamics and significance of those relationships, you may still wish to answer these questions. However, if you have any doubts about how and where your low self-esteem developed, it is strongly suggested that you work through the following exercises slowly and thoughtfully. If a question doesn't pertain to you, e.g., were your parents divorced, move on to the next applicable question.

3D-1. Describe your siblings. List the names and current ages of your brother, sisters, half-brothers, and half-sisters from oldest to youngest.

_____

_____

_____

_____

_____

_____

_____

_____

3D-2. If your parents were divorced, which of your siblings did you live with?

_____

_____

_____

_____

_____

_____

_____

_____

3D-3. Were you afraid of any of your siblings? Who? Explain why.

_____

_____

_____

_____

_____

- Were your parents aware that you were afraid of that particular sibling? If so, did they see to it that you weren't left alone with that person?

_____

_____

_____

_____

3D-4. Did any of your siblings ever hurt you or mistreat you badly? Did they ridicule you at home or school? If your parents knew about this, did they do anything to discipline or punish that sibling? Was it effective? Did the problem stop? Did you continue to be afraid?

_____

_____

_____

_____

_____

_____

_____

3D-5. Were any specific incidents between you and a sibling particularly painful? If so, describe them. Did anyone else know about these incidents? Was anything done to intervene so that this behavior was not repeated?

_____

_____

_____

_____

_____

_____

_____

_____

_____

_____

_____

3D-6. Were any of your siblings especially popular, enterprising, athletic, intelligent? How did this affect you? Did you feel inferior because of their advanced skills and abilities?

_____

_____

_____

_____

3D-7. Were you jealous of any of your siblings? Do you think any of your siblings were jealous of you? Explain.

_____

_____

_____

_____

3D-8. Did any one or more of your siblings have serious health problems? If so, how did this affect your life?

_____

_____

_____

_____

3D-9. Write the name of each sibling and behind each name write words or a phrase that best describes the emotional health of each one at this present time. For instance, are they stable, unstable, depressed, fully functioning, troubled, seriously mentally ill?

_____

_____

_____

_____

_____

_____

_____

_____

_____

_____

- In 3D-9 above, write the letters "LSE" behind the name of each sibling whom you believe has low self-esteem.

- In 3D-9 above, circle the names of those with whom you currently have a good relationship.

3D-10. Were any of your siblings in trouble at home or outside the home? With the law? At school? Within the community? Explain.

- Were you ever in trouble at home or outside the home? Explain.

_____

_____

_____

_____

_____

_____

_____

3D-11. If you answered yes to either of the questions in 3D-10 above, how did your parents react and what did they do? For example, did they listen to the explanation of the accused child (whether you or a sibling)? Did they defend the actions of that child? Did they support the discipline applied by the school or the ruling of courts? Always? Never? Explain.

_____

_____

_____

_____

_____

_____

_____

_____

_____

_____

_____

_____

_____

- Did they apply discipline or punishment of their own? What type of punishment? At the time, did you think it was fair and appropriate? Do you still think so today?

_____

_____

_____

_____

_____

_____

• Select 3 words from the Feelings List that best describe how you felt then about the way your parents responded to these problems.

1._____

2._____

3._____

• How do you think these problems affected you at the time? What lasting effects do you think your problems or those of a sibling had on you?

_____

_____

_____

_____

_____

_____

_____

3D-12. How do you think these problems affected the family as a whole? Do you think it changed the dynamics or the ways in which your parents interacted with you personally?

_____

_____

_____

_____

_____

_____

• Select 3 words from the Feelings List that best describe how you felt about these changes.

1._____

2._____

3._____

3D-13. Were chores assigned to each of the siblings? If so:

• What were your chores?

_____

_____

_____

_____

• Did you feel that chores were assigned fairly to each child? If not, why not?

_____

_____

_____

_____

• Did all siblings generally complete their chores? If not, who didn't and why?

_____

_____

_____

_____

• Were there stated consequences for not completing these chores? Give examples.

_____

_____

_____

_____

• Were these consequences applied if the chores were not completed? Or were the consequences forgotten? Or were other unstated consequences applied instead?

_____

_____

_____

_____

• Did you feel that consequences were fairly applied to each child who did not complete his chores? Explain.

_____

_____

_____

_____

3D-14. Do you feel that either or both of your parents favored you or one or more of your siblings over the other children? Explain which parent did this, who they favored, in what ways they did so, and what impact you think this had on you and the family as a whole.

_____

_____

_____

_____

_____

_____

_____

_____

3D-15. Do you feel either or both of your parents specifically picked on, or singled out, you or one or more of your siblings in a negative way? Explain which parent did this, who they picked on, in what ways they did so, and what impact you think this had on you and the family as a whole.

_____

_____

_____

_____

_____

_____

_____

_____

3D-16. Describe any other memories you have concerning your siblings or your relationships with them that you feel may have impacted your low self-esteem.

_____

_____

_____

_____

_____

_____

_____

_____

Recap of "The impact and behavior of my siblings": *After rereading your responses to this section, are you now aware of anything that might have contributed to the development of your low self-esteem?*

_____

_____

_____

_____

_____

_____

_____

_____

_____

_____

_____

_____

_____

_____

_____

_____

_____

_____

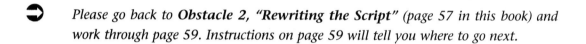

*Please go back to **Obstacle 2, "Rewriting the Script"** (page 57 in this book) and work through page 59. Instructions on page 59 will tell you where to go next.*

Obstacle 3, Excursion E

Living in a Blended or Single-parent Family

> Authors note: If you did not come from a blended or single-parent family you may want to skip over this section and move directly to Obstacle 3, Excursion F.

Even more complicated than nuclear family interactions are the family dynamics that are present within the blended family. In these homes, where many possible combinations are present, children may come and go on weekends or during the week and each child may live with one biological parent and one stepparent plus additional children by the stepparent's former relationships. Additionally, some of the children may be the product of both parents and reside in the home at all times while their half-sisters and half-brothers come and go. Even in the best of circumstances, where the non-custodial parent is stable, cooperative, and has in mind the best interests of the child, these arrangements can produce problems. For instance, if the discipline and rules in one home are very different from what they are in the other, children have to emotionally shift gears to adjust to each move between environments. Differences in personality, life-style, atmosphere of the home, expectations of the individual adults, and the economic level of the parents can have a profound effect on the degree of adjustment that must be made each time a child leaves and enters one of the households. What's more, the child may be expected to interact with and develop a significant relationship with a stepparent.

Situations in which children move back and forth between a single-parent household and a household of parent plus stepparent can have these same and additional dynamics. Sometimes children come home to a single-parent household and feel guilty telling that parent how good a time they had with the other parent; they may think this makes their single-parent feel alone and lonely. Additionally children in single-parent households may feel their parent doesn't have enough time for them, because the single parent has to do all of the work without another adult to share the load. On the other hand, children of single-parent households may need to share more responsibilities and have less time to get into trouble or may get as much or more attention because the single-parent doesn't need to focus on a partner. Parent and children may also put forth more effort to work together in running the household out of necessity.

Obviously, the possible scenarios are too many and varied to cover here; these are but a few possible obstacles that can present challenges within blended and one-parent households. Hopefully, beginning to think about the issues presented here will stimulate your thinking about the issues that might have influenced your early life and your view of yourself. With that in mind, answer the following:

3E-1. Did you live with both of your **biological** parents throughout your childhood? If not, which parent did you live with and for how long?

_____

_____

_____

_____

_____

_____

3E.2. Concerning your **non-custodial parent**:

- How often and for what periods of time did you see your non-custodial parent?

_____

_____

_____

_____

_____

_____

- Select 3 words from the Feelings List that best describe how you felt about the time you spent with your non-custodial parent. If your feelings changed at different periods, explain those changes and select words for each period of time.

1._____

_____

_____

2._____

_____

_____

3._____

_____

_____

3E-3. Describe the relationship (as best you remember it from your youth) between your custodial parent and non-custodial parent.

• Were they civil toward each other? If not, did they involve you (and the other children) in their disagreements?

_____

_____

_____

_____

_____

_____

• Did either of them try to influence your feelings about the other biological parent or stepparent? If so, explain what they did and how this affected you.

_____

_____

_____

_____

_____

_____

• Choose 3 words from the Feelings List or phrases of your own that best describe how you felt about how the interactions between your custodial and non-custodial parent. For instance, did they frighten you? Did they disgust you? Did you dread times when they both were present?

1._____

2._____

3._____

3E-4. If your parents were divorced and your **custodial parent** remarried, describe the relationship you had with your custodial stepfather or stepmother.

- Did you feel comfortable with your custodial stepparent? Why or why not?

_____

_____

_____

_____

_____

_____

_____

_____

- Did you feel you were supported, encouraged, affirmed by your custodial stepparent? Explain.

_____

_____

_____

_____

_____

_____

- Did you feel that your custodial stepparent was emotionally available to you? To listen to you? To take an interest in what you were doing and learning at school and with your friends? Give examples.

_____

_____

_____

_____

_____

_____

- Did you or do you now feel that your custodial stepparent interfered with your relationship with your biological, custodial parent? Give examples.

_____

_____

_____

_____

_____

_____

- Did any particular problems arise out of your relationship with your custodial stepparent? Give examples.

_____

_____

_____

_____

_____

_____

- Choose 3 words from the Feelings List that best describe how you felt about your custodial stepparent.

1._____

2._____

3._____

3E-5. If your parents were divorced and your **non-custodial parent** remarried, describe the relationship you had with your non-custodial stepparent.

- Did you feel comfortable with your non-custodial stepparent? Why or why not?

_____

_____

_____

_____

_____

_____

_____

_____

_____

_____

- Did you feel supported, encouraged, affirmed by your non-custodial stepparent? Why or why not?

_____

_____

_____

_____

_____

_____

- Did you feel that your non-custodial stepparent was emotionally available to you? To listen to you? To take an interest in your school achievement, your activities, your friends? Give examples.

_____

_____

_____

_____

_____

_____

- Did you or do you now think that your non-custodial stepparent interfered with your relationship with your biological, non-custodial parent? If so, how?

_____

_____

_____

_____

_____

_____

_____

_____

_____

• Did any particular problems arise out of your relationship with your non-custodial stepparent? Explain.

_____

_____

_____

_____

_____

_____

_____

_____

• Choose 3 words from the Feelings List that best describe how you felt about your non-custodial stepparent.

1._____

2._____

3._____

3E-6. Describe any additional negative situations or events that occurred as a result of living and moving between two households, as a result of interacting with custodial and non-custodial parents and stepparents, or as a result of the interactions between your custodial and non-custodial parents and stepparents.

_____

_____

_____

_____

_____

_____

_____

_____

_____

_____

_____

_____

_____

_____

3E-7. If your non-custodial parent was seldom involved in your life, or was involved inconsistently, how did this affect you?

_____

_____

_____

_____

3E-8. Choose 3 words form the Feelings List that best describe how you felt about your with your custodial parent. Feel free to use your own words or phrases.

    1._____

    2._____

    3._____

3E-9. If your parents were divorced and your non-custodial parent did not regularly spend time with you, explain how this affected you.

    •   Did you think it was your fault your parents divorced? Did you think the absent parent didn't love you? Were you confused? Were you angry?

_____

_____

_____

_____

_____

_____

_____

_____

_____

- Did you blame your custodial parent for the absence of the other parent? Did this affect your relationship with your custodial parent?

_____

_____

_____

_____

- What long-range effect do you think the absence of your non-custodial parent had on you? On your self-esteem?

_____

_____

_____

_____

3E-10. Describe any other relevant, negative information or incidents that you feel resulted from being raised in a single-parent family.

_____

_____

_____

_____

3E-11. Explain any other relevant, negative information or incidents that you feel resulted from your parents' divorce or from the additional people and circumstances that came into your life following the divorce.

_____

_____

_____

_____

_____

_____

Recap of "The ramifications of living in a blended or single-parent family":
After rereading your responses to this section, are you now aware of anything about your blended family or single-parent home life that might have contributed to the development of you low self-esteem?

_____

_____

_____

_____

_____

_____

_____

_____

_____

_____

_____

_____

_____

_____

➲   *Please continue on to the next page (154) and work through page 161.*

Obstacle 3, Excursion F

Additional People Who Lived in My Home

Additional people who lived in your home during the first few years of your life may also have played a significant role in the development of your low self-esteem. An ill grandparent or aunt may have taken up a considerable amount of one or both parent's time leaving you feeling neglected, abandoned, or inconsequential. A relative who was financially irresponsible or recovering from some tragedy might have placed a burden on the family that translated into short tempers, arguments, and tension that created fear and uncertainty in you. An abusive friend or relative may have criticized you or treated you badly, resulting in you wondering why your parents allowed this to happen and why they didn't protect you. An immature or rebellious person may have encouraged you to do drugs or involved you in some other inappropriate behavior for which you were later severely punished or from which you have emotional scars. Move on now to these questions.

3F-1. Did any other people live in your home during your childhood, preadolescence, or teen years?

- Who, when, and for how long?

_____

_____

_____

_____

_____

_____

- What was the relationship of this person to the family, e.g., elderly or other relative, friend, adopted child, foster child?

_____

_____

_____

• To the best of your knowledge, why was this person living in your home?

_____

_____

_____

_____

• Did the presence of this person create any problems for the family or require any special care?

_____

_____

_____

_____

• Did this person's presence create any difficulties for you personally? For example, did you have to give up your bedroom? Was this person abusive? Was this person demanding?

_____

_____

_____

_____

_____

_____

3F-2. Did you have frequent visitors who stayed for long periods of time, thus negatively impacting you or your family? Explain.

_____

_____

_____

_____

_____

3F-3. Describe any additional negative interactions or specific incidents you remember that were the result of the presence of others living or visiting in your home.

_____

_____

_____

_____

_____

_____

Recap of "Additional people who lived in my home": *In reviewing your responses to this section, are you now aware of anything stemming from this information about others who lived in your home that might have contributed to the development of your low self-esteem? If so, explain.*

_____

_____

_____

_____

_____

_____

_____

_____

_____

_____

➲   *Please continue on to the next page (157) and work through page 161.*

Obstacle 3, Excursion G

Illness of Family Members

Living with those who are seriously ill can be very frightening for young children. All too often adults do not explain to children what is happening, leaving the children to worry that the ill person is going to die, leaving them to wonder if they might catch the disease and become ill themselves, and leaving them confused and uncertain about what the future holds. Believing they should shield their children, these well-meaning parents withhold information that could quell children's fears and provide them with some predictability. Without such information, children's imaginations are left to run rampant, creating irrational scenarios and broad insecurity.

3G-1. Did anyone in your immediate family have serious health problems? If so:

- Was this a parent? A sibling? What was the duration of the illness and its outcome?

_____

_____

_____

- What was the nature of the illness and how much were you told at the time?

_____

_____

_____

_____

- How do you feel this illness affected you? For instance, were you frightened that the ill person would die?

_____

_____

_____

3G-2. What, if any, lasting effect do you think this had on you? For instance did you worry that something similar might happen to you? Did you worry that the person might become ill again?

_____

_____

_____

_____

3G-3. Did you ever witness this person having seizures, strokes, or attacks while they were at home? Describe how this affected you.

_____

_____

_____

_____

3G-4. Were you often left alone while your parents were at the hospital? Were they often gone to the doctor's office or attending to the needs of the ill person? What did you do while this was happening?

_____

_____

_____

_____

• Were babysitters or relatives often in charge of the family during these times? If so, was this a positive or negative experience?

_____

_____

_____

_____

_____

_____

• Did you or an older sibling take over supervising the family? If so, did this cause problems between the siblings?

_____

_____

_____

_____

• Did anything bad happen while you were left alone or left with siblings or other family members? Explain.

_____

_____

_____

_____

• Did you have anyone to confide in, to talk to about your feelings, or to go to with your questions? Who were you able to turn to if neither parent was available? If you had someone to talk to, was this helpful?

_____

_____

_____

_____

_____

• Choose 3 words from the Feelings List that best describe how you felt when your parents were unavailable because they were attending to the ill person. For instance, were you worried, resentful, frightened? Did you feel abandoned or neglected? Did you feel alone?

1._____

2._____

3._____

3G-5. Explain how you think this illness affected the family dynamics and relation-ships between members of the family. For example, were your parents overly stressed and exhausted? Were they tense, irritable, or impatient? Were you or your siblings angry? Was anyone acting out?

_____

_____

_____

_____

_____

_____

_____

_____

3G-6. List the ways in which the family's normal routine was altered due to this illness.

_____

_____

_____

_____

_____

3G-7. Describe any other memories that you have connected to a family illness that you think might have impacted your self-esteem.

_____

_____

_____

_____

Recap of "Illness of family members": *Rereading your comments in this section, are you now aware of anything concerning the health and illness of a family member that may have contributed to your low self-esteem?*

_____

_____

_____

_____

_____

_____

_____

_____

_____

_____

_____

_____

_____

_____

_____

_____

_____

_____

_____

➡ *Please go back to **Obstacle 2, "Rewriting the Script"** (page 60 in this book) and work through page 69. Instructions on page 69 will tell you where to go next.*

Obstacle 3, Excursion H

The Environment in Which I Grew Up

The environment in which we grow up is composed of the people in it, the climate created by these people and their interactions, the setting, and the circumstances that affect us and the others in it. Whether or not we want to admit it, each of us is largely the product of our environment until or unless we make an effort to change some aspect of our lives that was formed by that environment. Thus, as mentioned before, much of what we think, including our views on religion, sex, and politics; many of our interests, whether in athletics, stamp collecting, or backpacking; and most of our attitudes, such as our views on the importance of education, a solid work ethic, or acceptance of others different from ourselves are primarily shaped by our environment.

Our environment also affects our view of self, for within this setting comes our first understanding of authority, of discipline, of rules, of a sense of family, and of a sense of self as it relates to others and as it fits into this environment and the world. What a child views and experiences in this environment is all she knows at first. Then as she steps out into the world and plays with neighbors, attends school, and accompanies her parents to different places, she begins to see a bigger stage, a bigger playing field. Still, once formed, her beliefs are hard to alter, her habits difficult to change, her views tough to transform. Such is the video tape of the person with low self-esteem, whose environment has recorded negative input about who she is, telling her she is unimportant, unwanted, unable to do things right, perhaps even a nuisance or a burden. Healthy environments generally breed healthy children and unhealthy environments breed unhealthy children, often children suffering from low self-esteem. Therefore, it is important to now focus on the environment in which you grew up to assess the ways in which that atmosphere and the circumstances that went with it affected you personally.

3H-1. Concentrating on the environment in which you grew up:

- When you were young, how did you compare your family to other families you knew? For example, did your family seem as close as other families, did your parents spend as much time with you as other parents seemed to spend with their children, did your mother work while your friend's mothers were always home, was your family involved in similar activities as other families, did they entertain more or less than other families you knew, did your parents seem to argue more than the parents of your friends? Describe the similarities and differences.

_____

_____

_____

_____

_____

_____

_____

_____

_____

_____

_____

_____

_____

_____

_____

_____

_____

_____

•   In looking back, how do you <u>now</u> think your family of origin compared with others you knew? For example, was yours more or less dysfunctional? Explain your thoughts and what, if any, negative effects you think this had on your view of yourself.

_____

_____

_____

_____

_____

_____

_____

_____

_____

_____

_____

• How would you describe the climate or atmosphere of your home when you were growing up? Was it warm and loving? Tense? Hostile? Chaotic? Explain.

_____

_____

_____

_____

_____

_____

_____

• Choose 3 words from the Feelings List that best describe how you felt when you were at home or with members of your family. Feel free to use your own words or phrases.

1._____

2._____

3._____

• Did the atmosphere in your home change at any point when you were growing up? If so, what do you think caused this change? For example, did your mother quit drinking? Did your father lose his job? Did your sister get pregnant? Did one of your parents have an affair?

_____

_____

_____

_____

_____

_____

• Did this change make life at home better or worse? Give examples.

_____

_____

_____

_____

_____

_____

3H-2. Do you remember feeling secure and safe in your home, in the home of friends and relatives and in your community? Explain.

• As a child

_____

_____

_____

_____

• As a preadolescent

_____

_____

_____

_____

_____

• As a teenager

_____

_____

_____

_____

_____

_____

3H-3. Was there anyone in particular who you were afraid of? Explain who and why.

_____

_____

_____

_____

_____

_____

3H-4. If you did not feel safe at home, was there anyone you could and did tell about this? If so, did this bring you any comfort or did it help in any way?

_____

_____

_____

_____

3H-5. How do you think your family's economic standing compared with other families within the community?

• Did your parent's income seem to closely match that of the families of your friends, fellow students, neighbors, and other relatives? If not, do you think your parents had more or less money than these other families? Explain.

_____

_____

_____

_____

_____

_____

_____

_____

_____

_____

_____

- Were you aware of any specific problems concerning money?

_____

_____

_____

_____

- Did your parents discuss money issues or argue about money in your presence? Explain.

_____

_____

_____

_____

3H-6. If there was a significant difference in the financial resources of your family compared to that of your friends, relatives, and neighbors:

- What effect, if any, do you think that had on you? Did you feel deprived in any way? Did you have to work while your friends did not? Were you unable to dress as well as your friends? Were you unable to attend the college of your choice or any college at all?

_____

_____

_____

_____

_____

_____

_____

_____

- If you had less money and fewer opportunities than others, choose 3 words from the Feelings List that best describe how you felt about the situation. If you didn't have less money than others, move on to the next question.

1._____

2._____

3._____

- If you had more money than others and were aware of it, choose 3 words from the Feelings List that best describe how you felt as a result.

1._____

2._____

3._____

- What effect, if any, do you think your parents' financial resources or lack thereof had upon how you felt about *them*? For example, did you think that your family's lack of finances was due to your father's inability to keep a job or lack of ambition? Did you feel bad for a parent because you felt that parent had been treated unfairly or had been unable to afford an education for himself?

_____

_____

_____

_____

_____

_____

_____

• What effect, if any, do you think your family's economic situation had on how others viewed you and your family?

_____

_____

_____

_____

_____

_____

• Describe any negative incidents that occurred as a result of your parents' lack of adequate financial resources.

_____

_____

_____

_____

_____

_____

• Describe any other problems that you feel were related to financial resources or lack thereof or any other specific feelings you had about the subject.

_____

_____

_____

_____

_____

_____

_____

3H-7. Did your family have any "secrets" or unspoken problems that you were aware of at the time, even if they weren't openly acknowledged (e.g., alcoholism, incest, mental health issues, gambling, extramarital affairs, domestic violence, trouble with the law)?

- What were the "secrets" and who had them?

_____

_____

_____

_____

_____

_____

_____

_____

- How and at what age did you become aware of this?

_____

_____

_____

_____

_____

_____

- Did any of these problems directly impact you? Give examples.

_____

_____

_____

_____

_____

_____

_____

_____

_____

• How was the behavior around these problems explained, kept hidden, or rationalized?

_____

_____

_____

_____

_____

_____

_____

_____

3H-8. Did your family have any secrets or unspoken problems that you were NOT aware of at the time but which you now know about? Have these "secrets" ever been openly acknowledged? Explain what they were and how you became aware of them.

_____

_____

_____

_____

_____

_____

_____

_____

_____

_____

_____

_____

_____

3H-9. If your family had secrets, what effect do you NOW think these had on the family as a whole and its members individually? What effect, if any, do you NOW think these secrets had on you? Explain in as much detail as you can.

_____

_____

_____

_____

_____

_____

_____

_____

_____

_____

_____

_____

_____

3H-10. Were you ever left with babysitters? Describe any situations that were particularly negative.

_____

_____

_____

_____

_____

_____

_____

_____

_____

3H-11. During your school years, was a parent there to pick you up at school or at home to greet you? If so, describe the interaction that usually took place between you and that parent.

_____

_____

_____

_____

_____

_____

_____

_____

3H-12. If parents were not available after school:

• Where did you go and what did you do?

_____

_____

_____

_____

_____

• Who was in charge at home or were you on your own?

_____

_____

• Was this a positive or negative situation for you? For instance were you lonely, bored, frightened? Or did you enjoy having some time to yourself to read, study, or listen to music?

_____

_____

_____

_____

_____

_____

• Did you have friends visit at your home while your parents were gone? If so, did you ever get in trouble during those times or do things you knew you shouldn't be doing? Explain.

_____

_____

_____

_____

_____

_____

• Did any negative situations occur as a result of being at home without adult supervision following the school day?

_____

_____

_____

_____

_____

_____

_____

3H-13. Did your family frequently spend time together at home or regularly engage in family outings? If so, what type of activities did you do as a family? Did you go biking or hiking, on picnics, play table games, visit relatives? Did you attend sporting events, movies, concerts, fairs, or other community functions? List these and explain how often these outings or family events occurred and who was generally involved.

_____

_____

_____

_____

_____

_____

_____

_____

_____

_____

_____

_____

3H-14. Were these outings generally positive events? Were they fun or did they often turn sour in some way? For example, did they end with people being nasty or argumentative? Did they end with people complaining and unhappy? Explain.

_____

_____

_____

3H-15. Choose 3 words from the Feelings List that describe how you felt about family outings.

1._____

2._____

3._____

3H-16. Did your family take vacations together?

- If so, where did you go? How often? If not, why not?

_____

_____

_____

- Do you have good memories of these times? Explain why or why not.

_____

_____

_____

_____

_____

_____

_____

_____

- Choose 3 words from the Feelings List that describe how you felt about family vacations.

1._____

2._____

3._____

3H-17. Did you and your siblings feel safe in sharing your ideas and opinions or even disagreements within the family? Was this type of communication encouraged or discouraged? Give examples.

_____

_____

_____

_____

_____

_____

_____

_____

_____

3H-18. When you were young, do you remember any behaviors, practices, habits, or beliefs that your parents held or practiced that you thought were unusual or abnormal? Did they never invite company to your home? Did they refuse to clean the house? Did they have affairs? Did they have difficulty keeping jobs? Did they belong to a cult? Did they make their income by doing things that were against the law?

_____

_____

_____

_____

_____

_____

_____

_____

_____

_____

•   Is there anything that you NOW realize was unusual or abnormal about your family that you didn't recognize then? Explain what it was and how you now think it affected you and the family as a whole.

_____

_____

_____

_____

_____

_____

_____

_____

_____

3H-19. Do you remember periods of time when you were particularly unhappy, sad, depressed, afraid or lonely? Describe when these were, what you felt, and what you think was happening in your life or in the lives of members of your family at that time.

_____

_____

_____

_____

_____

_____

_____

_____

_____

_____

NOTE: The neighborhood and community in which you spent your early years will have affected your perspective on many issues as they were a part of the environment in which you grew up. If, for instance, you lived in a racially diverse area, you may be more or less tolerant of others who are different from yourself, depending on whether your interactions with others in that community were of a positive or negative nature. Your views on politics, religion, careers, family traditions and rituals, and future expectations about your life may have largely been shaped by your neighborhood and the people who you interacted with there during your developmental years.

Below, think back on those years and attempt to recapture the general flavor and specific events that you think might have played into the development of your LSE.

3H-20. Describe the community in which you grew up. If there were several, choose the one that you think had the most effect on your thinking and about how you feel about yourself.

• Was it a diverse community? Were different races represented? If so, was your own race the most prominent? If not, which race was? Was this an issue or problem for you and your family?

_____

_____

_____

_____

_____

• Was your community one that encouraged independence, career, and getting ahead in life? Or was it of a depressed and discouraged mentality, where people felt hopeless about the future and without resources, and where they never made an attempt to better themselves? Explain.

_____

_____

_____

_____

• Was there anything particularly strange about the community you grew up in? For instance, was it a commune, part of a cult, or another group with extreme beliefs? Were there other unusual circumstances? Was it a military base? Were your parents missionaries in a foreign land? Were you illegal immigrants? If so, describe the group and circumstances and how you think it affected you at the time and your ability to later fit into more normal living.

_____

_____

_____

_____

_____

_____

• Do you think your community in any way helped shape your negative self-esteem? If so, how?

_____

_____

_____

_____

_____

_____

3H-21. Were there individuals in your neighborhood or community that especially caused you problems or who did something to you that contributed to your negative view of yourself? If so what did they do and how did it affect your life?

_____

_____

_____

_____

_____

_____

3H-22. Did any traumatic events happen to you in your neighborhood or community? If so, describe what occurred.

_____

_____

_____

_____

_____

_____

■

Another part of the environment in which you grew up which were those people who fit into your extended family—relatives and close family friends who frequently interacted with you and others in your household. Each of these people likely had an impact on your life, some more than others, but an influence just the same. An uncle or grandmother who ridiculed you may have contributed to the bitterness and rage you now feel. A doting grandfather may have been the only person with whom you felt safe. A relative or family friend may have abused you sexually. A friend of your sibling may have introduced you to sex or drugs. A loving grandmother may have bolstered your self-esteem. Your mother's best friend may have encouraged and inspired you to go to college. Remembering who the significant people were in your life and how their presence affected you may provide a key to understanding how your low self-esteem was formed.

3H-23. About your extended family:

- Did any relatives or close family friends seem have a major influence on your parents? Do you think their influence was positive or negative? For instance, did a grandfather insist that your family maintain old family rituals or traditions? Were your parents financially dependent on other family members? Explain.

_____

_____

_____

_____

_____

_____

- Did the behavior, reputation, or status of any extended-family member have a memorable negative or positive affect on you or other members of your immediate family? Explain.

_____

_____

_____

_____

_____

_____

_____

_____

3H-24. Were you afraid of any members of your extended family? Explain who and why.

_____

_____

_____

_____

_____

_____

3H-25. Did one or more extended family members have a specific negative influence on you?

_____

_____

_____

_____

_____

_____

3H-26. Did any tragedies occur within the extended family that left a lasting affect on your life? Did someone die in a tragic way or at a young age? Was someone involved in a highly publicized scandal? Was anyone killed, kidnapped, or a witness to a serious crime? Did someone die of a rare disease? Did someone close to you run away or disappear and never return?

_____

_____

_____

_____

_____

_____

_____

3H-27. If such a tragedy did occur, how did this affect you at the time? How has it affected you since then?

_____

_____

_____

_____

_____

_____

3H-28. Describe anything else you remember about the environment in which you grew up that has not been addressed but that was of significance to your emotional development.

_____

_____

_____

_____

_____

_____

Recap of "The environment In which I grew up": *Rereading your comments in this section, are you now aware of anything concerning the environment in which you grew up that may have contributed to your low self-esteem?*

_____

_____

_____

_____

_____

_____

_____

_____

_____

_____

➲ *Please go back to **Obstacle 2, "Rewriting the Script"** (page 73 in this book) and work through page 75. Instructions on page 75 will tell you where to go next.*

Obstacle 3, Excursion J

My Education

Where we attended school and the conditions surrounding our early education may have fostered our low self-esteem. For instance, children whose parents are in the military or who, for some other reason, move frequently may have difficulty feeling comfortable or secure in school. After finally getting to know and understand the expectations of a teacher, they may have to move on to another school and another new teacher. Or they may begin and even excel in an activity in one community, then relocate to a town where that activity isn't offered, thus finding their lives continually disrupted.

Likewise, teachers who know of the family's transient lifestyle may not give as much attention to a child or even encourage her to begin long-range projects or join the soccer team, thinking that the family will likely leave before the project can be completed or before the soccer season ends. Teachers may feel that encouraging such activities is setting the child up for disappointment and discouragement.

In addition, the locale and quality of education we receive has a profound effect on our self-esteem. Growing up in a poor district where opportunities are few, the expectation for achievement is low, and encouragement is rare, a child's hope for life can easily be diminished, his motivation stifled. On the other hand, attending a quality school, being held in high regard by teachers, being the recipient of constant encouragement, praise, and respectful assistance can go a long way toward counterbalancing seriously, negative influences at home.

3J-1. How many schools did you attend when you were in:

- Elementary school? _____
- Junior high or middle school? _____
- Senior high school? _____

JUNKET 1: Elementary school
3J-2. Describe your experience of elementary school as you remember it.

- What did you like or dislike about it?

_____

_____

_____

_____

_____

_____

- How did you feel about your teachers? How did they treat you? Were they a positive or negative influence in your life? Was there one or more whom you particularly liked or disliked?

_____

_____

_____

_____

_____

_____

- How were your grades? Did you feel proud or ashamed of them? Did you care about your grades? Did your parents seem to care about them? How did they show they cared?

_____

_____

_____

_____

_____

_____

- What extracurricular activities were you involved in? Were you good, average, or poor at these activities? Was there one in particular that you enjoyed or excelled at?

_____

_____

_____

_____

• Choose 3 words from the Feelings List that describe how you felt about being involved in these activities. Feel free to use your own words or phrases.

1._____

2._____

3._____

• Were you anxious or frightened in elementary school or did you feel safe there? Explain.

_____

_____

_____

_____

_____

_____

• Was any particular incident during elementary school especially traumatic? Explain and tell how you think this incident affected you and you and your self-esteem.

_____

_____

_____

_____

_____

• Choose 3 words from the Feelings List that best describe how you felt about your elementary school experience.

1._____

2._____

3._____

JUNKET 2: Junior high or middle school

3J-3. Describe your experience of junior high or middle school as you remember it.

- What did you like or dislike about it?

_____

_____

_____

_____

_____

_____

- Were you a part of a group of kids who spent time together? How would you describe the group? Was it composed of the popular kids? The athletes? The intellectuals? The misfits?

_____

_____

_____

_____

_____

- Did you feel that you fit in or did you feel left out? If so, what do you believe caused you to feel that you fit in or to feel left out?

_____

_____

_____

_____

- How did you feel about your teachers? How did they treat you? Were they a positive or negative influence in your life? Was there one or more that you particularly liked or disliked?

_____

_____

_____

_____

_____

_____

- How were your grades? Did you feel proud or ashamed of them? Did you care about your grades? Did your parents seem to care about them?

_____

_____

_____

_____

_____

- Choose 3 words from the Feelings List that best describe how you felt about your academic performance.

1._____

2._____

3._____

- What extracurricular activities were you involved in? Were you good, average, or poor at these activities? Was there one in particular that you especially enjoyed or excelled at?

_____

_____

_____

_____

- Choose 3 words from the Feelings List that describe how you felt about being involved in these activities. Remember, you can always choose to use your own words or phrases.

1._____

2._____

3._____

• Were you anxious or frightened in junior high or middle school or did you feel safe there?

_____

_____

_____

_____

_____

• Was any particular incident during junior high/middle school especially traumatic? Explain.

_____

_____

_____

_____

_____

_____

• How do you think this incident affected you and your self-esteem?

_____

_____

_____

_____

• Choose 3 words from the Feelings List that best describe how you felt about your junior high/middle school experience.

1._____

2._____

3._____

JUNKET 3: Senior High School

3J-4. Describe your experience of senior high school as you remember it.

• Did you complete high school with others your age? Or have you completed your GED since becoming an adult? Explain

_____

_____

_____

_____

_____

• Did you like high school? What in particular did you like or dislike about it?

_____

_____

_____

_____

_____

_____

• Were you a part of a group of kids who spent a lot of time together? How would you describe the group? Was it composed of the popular kids? The athletes? The intellectuals? The misfits? What did you do together?

_____

_____

_____

_____

_____

_____

• Did you feel that you fit in or did you feel left out? What made you feel this way?

_____

_____

_____

_____

_____

- How did you feel about your teachers? How did they treat you? Were they a positive or negative influence in your life? Was there one or more that you particularly liked or disliked? Explain.

_____

_____

_____

_____

_____

_____

- How were your grades? Did you feel proud or ashamed of them? Did you care about your grades? Did your parents seem to care about them?

_____

_____

_____

_____

_____

_____

- Choose 3 words from the Feelings List that best describe how you felt about your academic performance.

1._____

2._____

3._____

- What extracurricular activities were you involved in? Were you good, average, or poor at these activities?

_____

_____

_____

_____

- Choose 3 words from the Feelings List that explain how you felt about being involved in these activities.

1._____

2._____

3._____

- Were you anxious or frightened in high school or did you feel safe there? Explain.

_____

_____

_____

_____

_____

- Choose 3 words from the Feelings List that best describe how you felt about your high school experience.

1._____

2._____

3._____

- Was any particular incident during high school especially traumatic? Describe the incident.

_____

_____

_____

_____

_____

_____

- How do you think this incident affected you and your self-esteem?

_____

_____

_____

_____

_____

_____

JUNKET 4: Overview of my education

3J-5. Over all, do you think you had a good education? Did the entire experience leave you feeling you had been successful or unsuccessful? Why?

_____

_____

_____

_____

_____

3J-6. Were your parents involved in your school progress? In what way? Did they take an interest in your homework and whether you completed it? Did they help you with it? Did they take an interest in helping you select your classes as the beginning of each term?

_____

_____

_____

_____

_____

3J-7. Did your parents encourage you to continue your education in college or to seek special training?

_____

_____

_____

_____

3J-8. Do you think that your parents placed a low, medium, or high value on education? Explain why you think this.

_____

_____

_____

_____

3J-9. Was there anything about your family, your family's reputation in the community, or your family's economic status that affected the way you were treated at school? Explain.

_____

_____

_____

_____

3J-10. Over all, did you consider school to be a positive or negative part of your life? Explain.

_____

_____

_____

_____

3J-11. Did you follow in the footsteps of a sibling who was especially successful or unsuccessful? If so, explain the situation and how it affected you?

_____

_____

_____

_____

3J-12. Do you think the way you were treated by teachers and administrators or the way you were viewed by other students was in any way the result of the reputation of your siblings or your family within the community? Explain.

_____

_____

_____

_____

JUNKET 5: How I felt about myself as a student.

3J-13. Select 3 words from the Feelings List that best describe how you felt about your self as a student.

1._____

2._____

3._____

3J-14. Describe what do you think was the most difficult period in your school experience?

_____

_____

_____

_____

_____

_____

_____

_____

_____

_____

_____

Recap of "My Education": *In reviewing your responses to this section, are you now aware of anything stemming from your school experience that might have contributed to the development of your negative self-view?*

_____

_____

_____

_____

_____

_____

_____

_____

_____

_____

_____

_____

_____

_____

_____

_____

_____

_____

➲   *Please go back to **Obstacle 2, "Rewriting the Script"** (page 76 in this book) and work through page 78. Instructions on page 78 will tell you where to go next.*

Obstacle 3, Excursion K

My Mother and My Relationship with Her

Mother-child relationships are very complex, especially when the mother in question is unhealthy. Girls especially are often more closely aligned with their mother's interests and generally in the company of their mothers more than with their fathers, especially during their developmental years; and their view of themselves is largely dependent on the maturity, parenting skills, emotional stability, attitudes, and contentment of their mothers with themselves and their own lives. Consequently, mothers who are unhappy, self-focused, and critical, and who withhold approval often raise daughters who are insecure, unhappy, critical of self and others, and who, in turn, withhold approval from others including their own children. Basically, mothers who are unhealthy and suffering from low self-esteem replicate their low self-esteem in their children.

Similarly, mother-son relationships can be especially detrimental if the mother is bitter and sees her son as a replica of the man who left her or disappointed her. She is also likely to raise a son with low self-esteem if she is overly critical because of her own feelings of inadequacy, or if she has unrealistic expectations, expects her son to satisfy her unmet needs, or for other reasons feels cheated in her life. Such unhealthy mothers often latch on to their sons so as to make them surrogate husbands. Others who see all men as weak, may treat their sons as invalids, creating unhealthy dependence, feelings of inadequacy, and either passivity or aggressiveness.

Thus, if a mother is stable, wants the best for her child, and is relatively happy, she is more likely to pass on a positive attitude. If, on the other hand, a mother is bitter, ill, unhappy, or has low self-esteem, she is less likely to raise a child with healthy self-esteem. Instead she may expect her children to fill the void in her life, she may be overly controlling as an attempt to feel secure, she may discourage independence because she fears being alone, and she may be very clingy because she is lonely and unable to get her needs met in constructive ways. On the other hand, she may go in the opposite direction and be too selfish to give her children the time and energy they need from her, seeing them and their activities as too much trouble. Either way, if your mother had low self-esteem, it is likely that she contributed to your having it as well. Whatever her personal qualities and failings, *being willing to see your mother for who she really was when you were young, will prove to be very important in your recovery.*

The purpose of the many questions in this set is to help you recollect specific aspects of your relationship with your mother. Obviously, we focus mostly on the negative aspects of this relationship because our goal is to ascertain if this relationship was instrumental in developing your low self-esteem. Examining the detrimental effects of this relationship in no way says that your mother did not have redeeming qualities nor does it mean she didn't love you or wasn't worthy of your love; most children, even those who have been severely abused by their parents, still love them. Instead this is an attempt to get at the truth about your developmental years and one of the primary influences on you during that time. Therefore, try not to be defensive about your mother, remembering that everyone has their strengths and weaknesses—it's just that certain weaknesses may have led to your LSE. If you feel you already know how your mother contributed to the development of your low self-esteem, you may not need to write out answers to all of the questions, but please read through them. If you have been unable to see how your mother contributed to your low self-esteem, you should answer all questions in detail, because all too often LSE begins in the home where the mother is a central figure.

NOTE: *If your mother was not present in your life when you were growing up, but another female was, such as a stepmother, grandmother, older sibling or aunt who served as one of your primary caregivers, these questions would apply to that person.*

3K-1. Did your mother have a job or career outside the home while you were growing up? During what periods of your life did she work outside the home? What type of work did she do?

_____

_____

_____

_____

_____

_____

3K-2. While your mother worked, who was in charge of childcare?

_____

_____

_____

_____

3K-3. What did your mother do around the home when she was there? Did she cook, clean, care for the children's needs, watch soap operas, sleep, talk on the phone?

_____

_____

_____

_____

_____

_____

3K-4. Did your mother have friends she spent time with on weekends or evenings? What type of activities did they engage in? How much was she away from home for these activities?

_____

_____

_____

_____

3K-5. If your mother did not have her own friends, why do you think that was?

_____

_____

_____

_____

3K-6. Did your mother take classes or belong to any civic, political, religious, or other organizations while you were growing up? If so, explain her role and time involvement in each.

_____

_____

_____

_____

_____

_____

_____

_____

3K-7. In relationship to your mother as a disciplinarian:

•   How did your mother discipline you? Were you disciplined often? In looking back, do you think her discipline was too severe or too lenient? Explain.

_____

_____

_____

_____

_____

_____

_____

_____

•   Do you feel your mother disciplined each of your brothers and sisters fairly and consistently? If not, who was more severely disciplined? Who was less severely disciplined? If your mother was inconsistent in her discipline, why do you think this was so?

_____

_____

_____

_____

_____

_____

_____

_____

3K-8. In looking back, do you think your mother was a healthy person when you were young?

•   Do you think she had emotional problems, physical problems, or personal issues that interfered with her ability to fulfill her responsibilities as a mother? If so, describe what you saw, what you remember, or what you now think about this issue. For example, was she under psychiatric care? Was she caring for an ailing parent? Was she in jail? Was her behavior bizarre in any way?

_____

_____

_____

_____

_____

_____

_____

_____

_____

•   Do you think now that your mother had low self-esteem? What makes you think this? What signs of LSE can you now associate with her behavior?

_____

_____

_____

_____

_____

_____

_____

_____

_____

_____

3K-9. Was your mother *overly* focused on her weight and appearance or the weight or appearance of you or your siblings? Give examples.

_____

_____

_____

_____

_____

_____

_____

_____

3K-10. Did you ever think that your mother was more concerned about her position in the community, what others thought about her, and how your behavior affected their opinions of her than she was about your feelings and personal development? Give examples.

_____

_____

_____

_____

_____

_____

_____

_____

_____

3K-11. Think about when you were younger,

- Did you feel you were close to your mother? Why or why not?

_____

_____

_____

_____

_____

_____

• In looking back, do you now think that you and your mother were emotionally close at any time while you were growing up? What makes you think this? In what ways were you close? Or if you now think that you weren't close, explain your thinking.

_____

_____

_____

_____

_____

_____

_____

_____

• Did your mother take an interest in your schoolwork, your activities, your friends? In what ways? Give examples.

_____

_____

_____

_____

_____

• If you were involved in school activities, did she attend those activities? How often? Did she attend parent-teacher conferences? If she attended your activities, what did she say afterwards? Did she compliment your performance? Did she criticize you? Was she just silent?

_____

_____

_____

_____

_____

_____

• Did you and your mother do activities together? Did she play with you? Explain.

_____

_____

_____

_____

• Did you have fun with her? Describe several specific times you remember having fun with your mother.

_____

_____

_____

_____

_____

_____

• Did she teach you new skills? If so, what skills? Was she patient or critical when doing this? Was she difficult to please?

_____

_____

_____

_____

_____

_____

• Did she talk to you about right and wrong and what is important in life? Did she take the time to explain things to you about people and relationships?

_____

_____

_____

_____

_____

_____

• How did your mother respond when you tried to talk about what was happening in your life or what was important to you? Could you share not only facts but also feelings with her? Give several examples of sharing such information with your mother and how she responded. Or, if you did not share such information with her, explain why.

_____

_____

_____

_____

_____

_____

_____

_____

_____

_____

_____

_____

_____

3K-12. Did you feel your mother was supportive of you? In what ways was she?

- As a small child

_____

_____

_____

_____

- As a preadolescent

_____

_____

_____

_____

_____

_____

- As a teenager

_____

_____

_____

_____

_____

_____

_____

- As an adult

_____

_____

_____

_____

_____

_____

_____

3K-13. Do you think she allowed you to be yourself and follow your own dreams or did she try to force you to do and be what she wanted? Give examples.

_____

_____

_____

_____

_____

_____

_____

3K-14. Do you think your mother was overly harsh, critical, or belittling? If so, describe incidents in which your mother did or said things that you still remember as particularly hurtful.

_____

_____

_____

_____

_____

_____

_____

_____

_____

3K-15. Was your mother more likely to verbalize approval or disapproval when you first suggested an opinion, shared a problem, or voiced an interest in doing something? Give three examples.

_____

_____

_____

_____

_____

_____

_____

_____

_____

_____

_____

3K-16. Are there ways in which your relationship with your mother has changed since you were young? If so, explain.

_____

_____

_____

_____

_____

_____

_____

_____

_____

3K-17. Looking back, do you think your mother was emotionally available to you?

- As child _____

- As a preadolescent _____
- As a teenager _____
- As a young adult _____

3K-18. Is your mother now emotionally available to you? If she is now elderly, or ill, or deceased, was she ever emotionally available to you as an adult? Give examples.

_____

_____

_____

_____

3K-19. Were you ever afraid of your mother? If so, why? Were you ever ashamed of her or something she did or said? Give examples.

_____

_____

_____

_____

_____

_____

_____

_____

3K-20. Do you think that your mother made every effort she could to protect you from harm? Explain why you think so.

_____

_____

_____

_____

_____

_____

_____

3K-21. Choose 3 words from the Feelings List that describe how you felt about your mother. Feel free to choose words or phrases of your own.

- As a child

_____

_____

_____

- As a preadolescent

_____

_____

_____

- As a teenager

_____

_____

_____

- Now as an adult

_____

_____

_____

3K-22. Do you think your mother was proud of you? Did she tell you so? Give an example of what you remember.

- As a child

_____

_____

_____

_____

- As a preadolescent

  _____

  _____

  _____

  _____

- As a teenager

  _____

  _____

  _____

  _____

- As a young adult

  _____

  _____

  _____

  _____

3K-23. Do you think she is proud of you today? Or, if she isn't living, do you think she was proud of you as you became an older adult? Explain why you think so.

_____

_____

_____

_____

_____

_____

_____

3K-24. If you do not feel your mother was proud of you when you were young, how do you think this affected you? Did you feel unimportant? Did you feel like a failure? Did you feel like there was no reason to achieve? Did you feel desperate to make her feel proud of you? What did you do?

_____
_____
_____
_____
_____
_____
_____
_____
_____
_____

3K-25. Do you feel your mother approved of you as a person? Of the choices you made? Of the way you dressed? Of your friends? Give examples.

- As a child

_____
_____
_____
_____

- As a preadolescent

_____
_____
_____
_____

- As a teenager

_____
_____
_____

_____

_____

_____

- As a young adult

_____

_____

_____

_____

_____

_____

3K-26. If she did not approve of something about you, e.g., your friends, or your choices, why do you think that was? Do you now think, for instance, that it was due to her own insecurities?

_____

_____

_____

_____

_____

_____

_____

_____

3K-27. If your mother consistently expressed disapproval of you, what you said and did, how you dressed, who your friends were, or anything else about you, how did this affect you? For instance, did you get discouraged and give up, did you get angry, did you try even harder to win her approval?

_____

_____

_____

_____

_____

_____

_____

_____

_____

_____

_____

_____

3K-28. How do you think her disapproval has affected you since your youth? Do you think it still has an effect on you today? Explain.

_____

_____

_____

_____

_____

_____

_____

_____

_____

_____

_____

3K-29. Did you feel loved by your mother?

- As a child _____

- As a preadolescent _____

- As a teenager _____

- As a young adult _____

3K-30. Do you remember your mother telling you that she loved you? Once? Occasionally? Frequently? Never?

- As a child _____

- As a preadolescent _____

- As a teenager _____

- As a young adult _____

- As an older adult _____

3K-31. Did you ever feel your mother had inappropriate expectations of you?
Did your mother treat you as a confidant, sharing her problems or frustrations with you when you were young? Did she do this with any of the other siblings?

_____

_____

_____

_____

- If she shared her problems with you, choose 3 words from the Feelings List that best describe how you felt when she did this.

1._____

2._____

3._____

- Did you ever think that it was your responsibility to take care of your mother, even though you were the child and she was the adult? Give two examples.

_____

_____

_____

_____

_____

_____

_____

_____

• Choose 3 words from the Feelings List that best describe how you felt about being responsible for her. Feel free to use you own words or phrases.

1._____

2._____

3._____

3K-32. Describe anything additional about your mother, her attitudes, her behaviors, her activities, or her background that you think is important to the development of your low self-esteem?

_____

_____

_____

_____

_____

_____

_____

_____

Recap of "My mother and my relationship with her": *In reviewing your responses to these questions, are you now aware of anything about your mother or your relationship with her that might have contributed to the development of your low self-esteem? Explain.*

_____

_____

_____

_____

_____

_____

_____

_____

_____

➲ *Please go back to **Obstacle 2, "Rewriting the Script"** (page 79 in this book) and work through page 84. Instructions on page 84 will tell you where to go next.*

Obstacle 3, Excursion L

My Father and My Relationship with Him

Generally, fathers have nearly as much opportunity and influence as mothers do to negatively affect their children's self-esteem; even fathers who are the primary childcare provider, because his work often removes him from the presence of his children more than is in their best interest.

Because traditionally fathers don't have as much daily interaction with their children as do mothers, the time they are available to their children is all the more important. If they work long hours but come home to take an interest in their children's school-work, friends, and activities, this attention will negate or at least reduce the effect of being gone so much. If fathers take time to play with their children, listen to them, teach them skills, affirm them, support and encourage them and are generous with praise and slow to criticize, this will effectively enhance healthy self-esteem.

If, on the other hand, fathers couple their many hours away from home with being emotionally distant when they are home, their children will feel devalued and abandoned. For instance, if they spend their few evening hours at home watching television, sleeping, or surfing the web, their children will feel ignored and insignificant. If fathers spend their weekends fishing and playing golf with friends instead of with their children, the children will feel unimportant. If a father drinks and mistreats his children or their mother, they will feel afraid of him; they may also feel unwanted or a disappointment. If he divorces their mother and then doesn't come to see them regularly, they will feel neglected, unworthy, and depressed, always wondering what is wrong with them.

Children look up to their parents for leadership and approval. When that approval is combined with loving attitudes and supportive behaviors, children develop confidence in themselves and in their ability to tackle future challenges. When children are proud of their parents, they feel more secure in who they are. When they are ashamed of their parents, they feel frightened and unsure about who they are themselves.

Whatever the circumstances were in your home, it's important now to truthfully assess who your father was, how effective he was as a parent, and how your relationship with him affected your personal view of yourself. *Remember the goal of this exercise is to determine the truth about your relationship with your father and whether his behavior contributed to your low self-esteem, so that you can then move toward overcoming this problem; it is not an exercise in demeaning your father and does not suggest you should not love him.*

> **NOTE:** *If your father was not present in your life when you were growing up, but another male was, such as a stepfather, grandfather, older sibling, or uncle who served as one of your primary caregivers, these questions would apply to that person.*

3L-1. Did your father have a job or career outside the home while you were growing up? During what periods of your life did he work outside the home? What type of work did he do?

_____

_____

_____

_____

_____

_____

_____

_____

_____

_____

3L-2. What did your father do around the home when he was there? Did he do his share of the cooking, cleaning, and childcare or did he mostly watch football, work in the yard, or sleep?

_____

_____

_____

_____

_____

_____

3L-3. Did your father have friends he spent time with on weekends or evenings? What type of activities did they engage in? How much was he away from home for these activities?

_____

_____

_____

_____

3L-4. If your father did not have his own friends, why do you think that was?

_____

_____

_____

_____

3L-5. Did your father take classes or belong to any civic, political, religious, or other organizations while you were growing up? If so, explain his role and time involvement in each.

_____

_____

_____

_____

_____

_____

_____

3L-6. How did your father discipline you?

• Were you disciplined often? In looking back, do you think his discipline was too severe or too lenient? Give examples.

_____

_____

_____

_____

_____

_____

_____

• Do you feel your father disciplined each of your siblings fairly and consistently? If not, who was more severely disciplined? Who was less severely disciplined? If your father was inconsistent in his discipline, why do you think this was so?

_____

_____

_____

_____

_____

_____

_____

_____

_____

_____

3L-7. In looking back, do you think your father was a healthy person when you were young?

• Do you think he had emotional problems, physical problems, or personal issues that interfered with his ability to fulfill his responsibilities as a father? If so, describe what you saw, what you remember, or what you now think about this issue. For example, was he under psychiatric care? Was he working at extra jobs to keep up with the bills? Did he gamble? Was he in jail? Give examples.

_____

_____

_____

_____

_____

_____

_____

_____

_____

_____

• Do you think now that your father had low self-esteem? What makes you think this? What signs of LSE can you now associate with his behavior?

_____

_____

_____

_____

_____

_____

_____

_____

_____

3L-8. Was your father *overly* focused on his weight or his appearance or the weight or appearance of you or your siblings? Give examples.

_____

_____

_____

_____

_____

_____

_____

3L-9. Did you ever feel that your father was more concerned about his position in the community, what others thought about him, and how your behavior affected their opinions of him than he was about your feelings and personal development? Explain your conclusions.

_____

_____

_____

_____

_____

_____

_____

_____

3L-10. Think about when you were younger,

• Did you feel you were close to your father? Why or why not?

_____

_____

_____

_____

_____

_____

• In looking back, do you now think that you and your father were emotionally close at any time while you were growing up? What makes you think this? In what ways were you close? Or if you now think that you weren't close, explain your thinking.

_____

_____

_____

_____

_____

_____

_____

_____

• Did your father take an interest in your schoolwork, your activities, your friends? In what ways?

_____

_____

_____

_____

_____

_____

• If you were involved in school activities, did he attend those activities? How often? Did he attend parent-teacher conferences? After activities, did your father comment on your performance? Did he criticize or praise your efforts? Or was he silent?

_____

_____

_____

_____

_____

• Did you and your father do activities together? Did he play with you? Describe this.

_____

_____

_____

• Did you have fun with him? Describe several specific times you remember having fun with your father.

_____

_____

_____

_____

_____

_____

_____

_____

- Did he teach you new skills? What skills? Was he patient or critical in teaching you new things? Was he difficult to please?

_____

_____

_____

_____

_____

- Did he talk to you about right and wrong and what is important in life? Did he take the time to explain things to you about people and relationships?

_____

_____

_____

_____

_____

- How did your father respond when *you* tried to talk about what was happening in your life or what was important to you? Could you share both facts and feelings with him? Give several examples of sharing such information with your father and how he responded. Or if you did not share such information with him, explain why.

_____

_____

_____

_____

_____

_____

_____

_____

_____

_____

_____

_____

_____

_____

3L-11. Did you feel your father was supportive of you? In what ways was he or wasn't he?

- As a small child

_____

_____

_____

_____

- As a preadolescent

_____

_____

_____

_____

_____

- As a teenager

_____

_____

_____

_____

_____

_____

_____

_____

- As an adult

_____

_____

_____

_____

_____

_____

_____

_____

3L-12. Did you think he allowed you to be yourself and follow your own dreams or did he try to force you to do and be what he wanted? Give examples.

_____

_____

_____

_____

_____

_____

_____

_____

3L-13. Did you think your father was overly harsh, critical, or belittling? If so, describe incidents in which your father did or said things that you still remember as particularly hurtful.

_____

_____

_____

_____

_____

_____

_____

_____

_____

_____

3L-14. Was your father more likely to verbalize approval or disapproval when you first suggested an opinion, shared a problem, or voiced an interest in doing something? Give three examples.

_____

_____

_____

_____

_____

_____

_____

_____

_____

_____

3L-15. Are there ways in which your relationship with your father has changed since you were young? If so, explain.

_____

_____

_____

_____

_____

_____

_____

_____

_____

3L-16. Looking back, do you think your father was emotionally available to you?

- As child _____

- As a preadolescent _____

- As a teenager _____

- As a young adult _____

3L-17. Is your father now emotionally available to you? Or if he is elderly, or ill, or deceased, was he ever emotionally available to you as an adult? Explain.

_____

_____

_____

_____

3L-18. Were you ever afraid of your father? If so, why? Were you ever ashamed of him or his behavior? Explain

_____

_____

_____

_____

_____

_____

_____

3L-19. Do you think that your father made every effort he could to protect you from harm? Explain why you think so.

_____

_____

_____

_____

_____

_____

3L-20. Choose 3 words from the Feelings List that describe how you felt about your father:

- As a small child

_____

_____

_____

- As a preadolescent

_____

_____

_____

- As a teenager

_____

_____

_____

- Now as an adult

_____

_____

_____

3L-21. Do you think your father was proud of you? Did he tell you so? Give an example of what you remember.

- As a child

_____

_____

_____

_____

- As a preadolescent

_____

_____

_____

_____

- As a teenager

_____

_____

_____

_____

- As a young adult

_____

_____

_____

_____

3L-22. Do you think he is proud of you today? Or, if he isn't living, do you think he was proud of you as you became an older adult? Explain why you think so.

_____

_____

_____
_____
_____
_____
_____
_____

3L-23. If you do not feel your father was proud of you when you were young, how do you think this affected you? Did you feel unimportant? Did you feel like a failure? Did you feel deflated? Did you feel like there was no reason to achieve?

_____
_____
_____
_____
_____
_____
_____
_____

3L-24. Did you feel your father approved of you as a person? Of the choices you made? Of the way you dressed? Of your friends? Explain.

- As a child

_____
_____
_____
_____

- As a preadolescent

_____
_____
_____

- As a teenager

_____

_____

_____

_____

_____

_____

- As a young adult

_____

_____

_____

_____

_____

3L-25. If he did not approve of something about you, your friends, or your choices, why do you think that was? Do you now think, for instance, that it was due to his own insecurities?

_____

_____

_____

_____

_____

_____

3L-26. Did you feel loved by your father?

- As a child _____
- As a preadolescent _____
- As a teenager _____
- As a young adult _____

3L-27. Do you remember your father telling you that he loved you? Once? Occasionally? Frequently? Never?

- As a child _____
- As a preadolescent _____
- As a teenager _____
- As a young adult _____
- As an older adult _____

3L-28. Did you ever feel your father had inappropriate expectations of you? Did he treat you as a confidant, sharing his problems or frustrations with you when you were young? Did he do this with any of the other siblings?

_____

_____

_____

_____

- If he shared his problems with you, choose 3 words from the Feelings List that best describe how you felt when he did this.

1._____

2._____

3._____

- Did you ever think that it was your responsibility to take care of your father, even though you were the child and he was the adult? Give two examples.

_____

_____

_____

_____

_____

_____

_____

• If so you felt it was your responsibility to take care of your father, choose 3 words from the Feelings List that best describe how you felt about being expected to b responsible for him.

1._____

2._____

3._____

3L-29. Describe anything additional about your father, his attitudes, his behaviors, his activities, or his background that you think is important to the development of your low self-esteem.

_____
_____
_____
_____
_____
_____
_____
_____

Recap of "My father and my relationship with him": *In reviewing your responses to these questions, are you now aware of anything about your father or your relationship with him that might have contributed to the development of your low self-esteem? Explain.*

_____
_____
_____
_____
_____
_____
_____
_____

_____

_____

_____

_____

_____

_____

_____

_____

_____

_____

_____

_____

_____

_____

_____

➲ *Please go forward to **Obstacle 4, "Catching Up"** (page 277 in this book) and work through page 279. Instructions on page 279 will tell you where to go next.*

Obstacle 3, Excursion M

My parents: How I Perceived Their Behavior and How I Felt About Them

The perspective we have of our parents as being honorable and respectable or dishonorable and an embarrassment has much to do with how we see ourselves. For instance, when we think of our parents as intelligent, honest and trustworthy; as having our best interests at heart; as stable and mature; and as respectful of others, we will likely respect them and want to be like them. Furthermore, if our parents demonstrate honesty and speak of the importance of being honest, we will likely accept this principle as one that's important to uphold.

If on the other hand we see our parents lying and cheating and then bragging about their gains, we may think that being dishonest and cutting corners has its rewards. Or we may grow up ashamed of that parent and feel we too must be flawed, or we may go to the other extreme and become rigid in our attempt to be totally honest. Furthermore, if our father was openly racist, we may either become racist ourselves or go to the other extreme of purposely choosing to form relationships with individuals of other races, parading them in front of him. In other words, we have likely either adopted the values, beliefs, and standards of our parents whether or not they were virtuous, or we have consciously or unconsciously reacted to what we saw, heard, and experienced and then developed opposing views and attitudes. Either way, without realizing it, our lives are often based on our positive or negative reactions to our parent's lifestyles, values, and attitudes.

> **NOTE:** *If your were raised by someone other than your parents, such as a grandmother, an older sibling, or an aunt and uncle, these questions would apply to whomever your caregivers were.*

3M-1. Were you proud of your mother, the kind of person she was and what she did and said?

- As a young child _____

- As a preadolescent _____
- As a teenager _____
- As a young adult _____

• If not, explain why and how this lack of pride in her affected how you felt about yourself. For instance, if you were ashamed of your mother, did you purposely avoid inviting your friends to your home? Did you refrain from asking her advice or sharing your problems with her?

_____

_____

_____

_____

_____

_____

_____

_____

_____

_____

3M-2. Were you proud of who your father was and what he did and said?

- As a young child _____
- As a preadolescent _____
- As a teenager _____
- As a young adult _____

• If not, explain why and how this lack of pride in him affected how you felt about yourself? For instance, did you purposely avoid telling him about your activities because you didn't want him to attend?

_____

_____

_____

_____

_____

_____

_____

_____

3M-3. Did you respect your mother?

- As a young child _____
- As a preadolescent _____
- As a teenager _____
- As a young adult _____

- If not, explain why and how did this lack of respect for her affected how you felt about yourself?

_____

_____

_____

_____

_____

_____

_____

_____

_____

3M-4. Did you respect your father?

- As a young child _____
- As a preadolescent _____
- As a teenager _____
- As a young adult _____

- If not, explain why and how did this lack of respect for him affected how you felt about yourself?

_____

_____

_____

_____

_____

_____

_____

_____

_____

_____

_____

3M-5. Did you think of your mother as a strong person? As a weak person? Explain.

_____

_____

_____

_____

_____

_____

_____

_____

3M-6. Did you think of your father as a strong person? As a weak person? Explain.

_____

_____

_____

_____

_____

_____

_____

_____

_____

NOTE: *Children tend to closely copy the behaviors and attitudes modeled by their parents and other significant adults, so how these people treated each other set the stage for your understanding—or lack thereof—of how intimate relationships work as well as your attitudes and beliefs about what to expect from others in relationships. For instance, if either of your parents were disrespectful of the other, you are more likely to be disrespectful of a partner yourself or to be tolerant when others are disrespectful of you. If your parents also treated you with disrespect, you likely developed self-doubts about yourself, including your worthiness to be loved. This will hold true unless and until you recognize that the attitude accompanying those behaviors is inappropriate AND you consciously choose to learn more appropriate ways to treat your partner than those you observed between your parents. If your parents were not openly loving and affectionate, you will be confused about whether or not such displays of affection are appropriate or even normal, and you may be reluctant to show affection to someone you really care about.*

If your parents were verbally, emotionally, or physically abusive to one another or if your father thought he should be the boss, you may have grown up replicating his behavior with your spouse (if you are male) or believe you should be submissive to a man (if you are female. Or, if your mother was unfaithful to your father, and you are male, you may think that women can't be trusted; if your father was unfaithful and you are female, you may think that it's okay for men "to play around." Such thoughts create confusion in children about what is and isn't appropriate behavior, and they create insecurity because children sense the tentative nature of the relationship.

Therefore, it's important not only to examine your observations of your parents' relationship with each other but also the attitudes that you developed about yourself and others as a result of witnessing your parents' behavior. In so doing, you will have a clearer view of how this has affected your view of yourself, your view of relationships, your expectations of others in relationships, and your level of trust in relationships.

3M-7. Do you think your parents had a loving and supportive relationship? Why do you think this?

_____

_____

_____

_____

_____

3M-8. If so, how did they demonstrate this?

- Did they hold hands, cuddle, or kiss in your presence? _____

- Did they tend to touch each other often in less intimate ways? _____

- Did they spend time together without other people? _____

- Did they talk often or for long periods of time? _____

- Did they laugh and smile when they were together? _____

- Did they compliment each other? _____

- Were they friendly and cordial to each other's friends? _____

- Were they sensitive to each other's feelings? _____

- Did they support each other's interests? Explain.

_____

_____

_____

_____

- Did they engage in activities together? Explain.

_____

_____

_____

_____

3M-9. Do you think your parents treated each other with respect? Give two examples.

_____

_____

_____

_____

_____

_____

3M-10. How do you think the way in which your parents treated each other has influenced how you treat others and how you expect them to treat you?

_____

_____

_____

_____

_____

_____

3M-11. Did your parents argue or fight in your presence? _____ If they went to their room to fight, could you hear what they were saying and doing? _____

•   Did their arguments involve yelling at each other? If so, who yelled? What did they say?

_____

_____

_____

_____

•   Did their arguments usually seem to get resolved? Was this because they reached an agreement or because one of them gave in to the demands of the other? Explain the patterns you observed then or recognize now.

_____

_____

_____

_____

•   Did either or both parents remain angry with each other for hours or days? Explain.

_____

_____

_____

_____

_____

_____

3M-12. What was the nature of their arguments?

- How often did they argue? What did they generally argue about?

_____

_____

_____

_____

_____

_____

- How often did these arguments become violent? What type of violent behavior did they display?

_____

_____

_____

_____

- Which was usually the violent person or were both parents violent?

_____

_____

_____

_____

- If only one of your parents became violent, what did the other parent do during the episode?

_____

_____

_____

_____

• Did either or both of your parents threaten divorce during these arguments? If so, how did these threats affect you?

_____

_____

_____

_____

_____

_____

• Was either alcohol or drug use involved in these arguments?

_____

_____

_____

_____

3M-13. To your knowledge, did your parents ever attend therapy because of these arguments or other problems in the marriage? Are you aware of their views on therapy?

_____

_____

3M-14. What did you and your siblings do when your parents argued? When they became violent?

_____

_____

_____

_____

3M-15. How do you feel your parents' violence affected you at the time?

_____

_____

_____

_____

_____

3M-16. Choose 3 words from the Feelings List that best describe the emotions you experienced when your parents argued. Feel free to use your own words or phrases.

   1._____

   2._____

   3._____

3M-17. Choose 3 words from the Feelings List that best describe the emotions you experienced when your parent or parents became violent. Feel free to use your own words or phrases.

   1._____

   2._____

   3._____

3M-18. How do you think your parent's patterns of arguing or violent behavior has affected how you have viewed relationships? For example, have you expected others to treat you in the same way? Have you been more tolerant of this type of behavior than may have been in your best interest?

_____

_____

_____

_____

_____

3M-19. Did your parents ever turn their violence onto the children? Which child? What form did the violence take? How did a typical incident end?

_____

_____

_____

_____

_____

_____

_____

_____

3M-20. How do you think these acts of violence toward you, a sibling, or a parent affected you at the time? What did you do? How do you think it has affected your self-esteem?

_____

_____

_____

_____

_____

3M-21. In spite of their problems, did you feel secure in the fact that your parents loved each other? Or were you fearful they would divorce? Did you wish they would divorce? Did this uncertainty create insecurity in you?

_____

_____

_____

_____

_____

_____

_____

3M-22. To your knowledge, did either of your parents have affairs when you were living at home? Which parent? How was this resolved? Did they divorce because of this?

_____

_____

_____

_____

_____

_____

3M-23. Choose 3 words from the Feelings List that describe how you felt about the lack of faithfulness of your parent(s)?

1._____

2._____

3._____

3M-24. How do you think your parents' affairs affected you and how you felt about yourself? How do you think these affairs affected your view of relationships and your expectations of others in relationships?

_____

_____

_____

_____

_____

_____

3M-25. Did either of your parents frequently use vulgar language? Was this ever directed at you? If so, how do you think this behavior affected your self-esteem?

_____

_____

_____

_____

3M-26. Select 3 words from the Feelings List that describe how you felt when your parent directed vulgar language toward you.

1._____

2._____

3._____

3M-27. Was one of your parents more educated than the other? If so, do you think this caused any problems between them? Give an example.

_____

_____

_____

_____

_____

_____

3M-28. Did you believe that your parents were honest people? Give examples.

_____

_____

_____

_____

_____

3M-29. Did you think that your parents practiced what they preached? Or was there a double standard for the children? How did this affect you? Give examples.

_____

_____

_____

_____

_____

_____

3M-30. How did your parents talk about or treat people of different races? Were they consistent in their attitudes or did they profess one thing in public and speak disparagingly of such others in private? Give examples.

_____

_____

_____

_____

_____

_____

3M-31. How did your parents talk about and treat people of different physical size, people from different economic backgrounds, or people with different levels of education? Give examples.

_____

_____

_____

_____

_____

_____

3M-32. How do you think you were affected by the way in which your parents talked about and treated others who were different from themselves?

_____

_____

_____

_____

3M-33. How much attention did each of your parents give to their own or each other's physical appearance?

- Father: About right? Obsessed? Too little? Explain.

_____

_____

_____

_____

- Mother: About right? Obsessed? Too little? Explain.

_____

_____

_____

_____

3M-34. How do you think you were affected by the views your parents had about physical appearance?

_____

_____

_____

_____

3M-35. Did your parents allow you to invite friends to your home? Did they encourage you to do so? Did you want your friends to come to your home? Were you embarrassed to bring friends to your home? If so, why?

_____

_____

_____

_____

_____

_____

_____

_____

_____

_____

3M-36. Select 3 words from the Feelings List that describe how you felt about bringing friends to your home.

1._____

2._____

3._____

3M-37. At the time, did you think your parents were good parents as compared to the parents of your friends?

_____

_____

_____

_____

3M-38. In review, how do you now view your parents as they were when you were growing up?

	Mother	Father
Were they:		
• good parents?	_____	_____
• loving?	_____	_____
• caring?	_____	_____
• supportive?	_____	_____
• emotionally available?	_____	_____
• physically available?	_____	_____
• controlling?	_____	_____
• self-absorbed?	_____	_____
• healthy?	_____	_____
• stable?	_____	_____
• mature?	_____	_____
• overly critical?	_____	_____
• abusive?	_____	_____
• respectable?	_____	_____
• honest?	_____	_____
• ambitious?	_____	_____
Did they:		
• allow me to be myself?	_____	_____
• tell me they were proud of me?	_____	_____

- tell me they loved me? _____ _____
- spend adequate time with me? _____ _____
- take time to teach me skills? _____ _____
- affirm me? _____ _____
- treat me with respect? _____ _____
- listen to me? _____ _____
- attend my activities? _____ _____
- have full lives of their own? _____ _____
- try to live their lives through me? _____ _____
- model appropriate behavior? _____ _____

3M-39. If you could have changed anything about the relationship you had with your father, or anything about how he behaved toward you, what would it have been?

- As a child

_____

_____

_____

- As a preadolescent

_____

_____

_____

- As a teenager

_____

_____

_____

_____

- As an adult

_____

_____

_____

_____

3M-40. If you could have changed anything about the relationship you had with your mother, or anything about how she behaved toward you, what would it have been?

- As a child

_____

_____

_____

- As a preadolescent

_____

_____

_____

- As a teenager

_____

_____

_____

_____

- As an adult

_____

_____

_____

_____

Recap of "My parents: how I perceived their behavior and how I felt about them": *In reviewing your responses to this section, are you aware of anything stemming from your parents' behavior, their relationship with each other, or your feelings about them that might have contributed to the development of your low self-esteem?*

_____

_____

_____

_____

_____

_____

_____

_____

_____

_____

_____

_____

_____

_____

_____

_____

_____

_____

➲ *Please go back to **Obstacle 2, "Rewriting the Script"** (page 85 in this book) and work through page 88. Instructions on page 88 will tell you where to go next.*

Obstacle 3, Excursion N

Summarizing This Exploration of My Childhood

You have just worked through twelve excursions as a way to remember and reflect on the many factors that contributed to your early development. These included focusing on the environment in which you grew up, the various people in your life then, the education you received, and the parents or other adults who trained you and who guided you through those years.

Many people who seek to recover from their low self-esteem are already cognizant of the incidents and patterns of behavior that led to their negative view of self and ultimately their deep-seated low self-esteem, but some people are not. Frequently they deny that there was anything negative in their childhood or at least they deny that there were incidents so severe as to have caused the problem they now grapple with. Of course, the main reason why people are unable to identify the source of their low self-esteem is that they lack information and understanding as to what causes LSE in the first place. And they don't understand how serious a problem it is to all those who have it or even what low self-esteem actually is. They often think that their problem is unique to them rather than a problem with specific, universal patterns common to millions of LSE sufferers. Once they become educated on these points, they become more amenable to the idea that the way a child is treated is the primary stimulus to the development of low self-esteem, rather than seeing it as a personal flaw. They begin to see the problem as one of cause and effect rather than something innately wrong with them; they become more willing to scrutinize their memories of childhood.

Another factor worth repeating, is the desire to see our parents or other authority figures as infallible. This encourages us to ignore their obvious personal problems, excuse their destructive behaviors, and justify their lack of emotional support by placing blame on ourselves. *This is the critical error of those with low self-esteem and the reason for this section. If we are unable to place the blame where it belongs, it lands back on ourselves. And until this inaccurate judgment can be corrected, we cannot overcome our LSE.* Conversely, once we recognize that we can consciously acknowledge our parents' failings and still love them, we become free to see them as human beings who have their shortcomings, who have made mistakes, and whose behaviors are subject to evaluation, like everyone else. It then becomes easier to look back and call a spade a spade, placing responsibility where it rightfully belongs: on those who treated us inappropriately.

The third issue that stands in the way of recognizing how our low self-esteem formed is the tendency to minimize the significance of one or more similar or unrelated past incidents in the formation of how we think and view ourselves today. We feel embarrassed to admit that we attached such great significance to the particular words or actions of others that they became the basis for our entire perspective on life. We want instead to rationalize that everyone has painful situations they have to deal with, everyone experiences rejection, everyone has disappointments and they don't all develop low self-esteem. So, what is wrong with us, we ask? Why have we been so seriously wounded by what is ordinary and common. The truth is that harsh words may be far too common, but they are not the norm. Abuse is all too frequent but totally inappropriate and harmful. Neglect is certainly prevalent but still inexcusable. And failing to give a child the love, affirmation, and support she needs, while widespread among the immature, the irresponsible, and the unhealthy, is a tragedy.

Hopefully, the explanations and exercises have helped you to pinpoint the experiences that marked the beginning of your negative view of self as well as the subsequent incidents that cemented that inaccurate and invalidating self-perception. Remember that just as it only takes one spark to start a fire, so too, LSE begins with one criticism, one rebuke, one rejection, or one abusive act. What then follows is what determines the direction a person's self-esteem takes.

While this expedition may have been extremely painful, bringing up long-forgotten memories that you wished could remain buried, the importance of your work here and its contribution to your recovery cannot be exaggerated. For if you now recognize events that contributed to your low self-esteem, you can also now begin to digest the fact that your LSE is an outgrowth of the behaviors of others toward you, rather than as the result of anything inherently wrong with you. In so doing, you can move to the next step: realizing that what has been learned (unfortunately and through no fault of your own) can be relearned and that what you have inaccurately believed to be the truth about you can be altered.

NOTE: Below, you are asked to summarize what you have learned and remembered that you believe to be pertinent to the evolution of your present level of self-esteem, whether mild, moderate, or severe. From time to time during your program of recovery, it may be necessary to review the answers you write in these following exercises.

3N-1. Describe up to 6 specific incidents from any time in your youth that you remember as being extremely painful and that you think played a role in how you view yourself today.

1st Incident (Write 2-3 sentences that summarize the incident.)

_____

_____

_____

_____

_____

_____

- Name the person or persons involved and their relationship to you.

_____

_____

- Rate the impact the incident had on you, by circling a number between 1 and 5 (5 = the most severe impact; 1 = the least severe).

    1   2   3   4   5

- Explain the negative effect this incident had on you at the time and in the subsequent years.

_____

_____

_____

_____

_____

_____

_____

2nd Incident (Write 2-3 sentences that summarize the incident.)

_____

_____

_____

_____

_____

_____

- Name the person or persons involved and their relationship to you.

_____

_____

- Rate the impact the incident had on you, by circling a number between 1 and 5 (5 = the most severe impact; 1 = the least severe).

      1   2   3   4   5

- Explain the negative effect this incident had on you at the time and in the subsequent years.

_____

_____

_____

_____

_____

_____

_____

_____

3rd **Incident** (Write 2-3 sentences that summarize the incident.)

_____

_____

_____

_____

_____

_____

• Name the person or persons involved and their relationship to you.

_____

_____

• Rate the impact the incident had on you, by circling a number between 1 and 5 (5 = the most severe impact; 1 = the least severe).

        1   2   3   4   5

• Explain the negative effect this incident had on you at the time and in the subsequent years.

_____

_____

_____

_____

_____

_____

_____

_____

4th Incident (Write 2-3 sentences that summarize the incident.)

_____

_____

_____

_____

_____

• Name the person or persons involved and their relationship to you.

_____

_____

- Rate the impact the incident had on you, by circling a number between 1 and 5 (5 = the most severe impact; 1 = the least severe).

1   2   3   4   5

- Explain the negative effect this incident had on you at the time and in the subsequent years.

_____

_____

_____

_____

_____

_____

_____

_____

5th Incident (Write 2-3 sentences that summarize the incident.)

_____

_____

_____

_____

_____

_____

- Name the person or persons involved and their relationship to you.

_____

_____

- Rate the impact the incident had on you, by circling a number between 1 and 5 (5 = the most severe impact; 1 = the least severe).

1   2   3   4   5

- Explain the negative effect this incident had on you at the time and in the subsequent years.

_____
_____
_____
_____
_____
_____
_____
_____

6th Incident (Write 2-3 sentences that summarize the incident.)

_____
_____
_____
_____
_____
_____

- Name the person or persons involved and their relationship to you.

_____
_____

- Rate the impact the incident had on you, by circling a number between 1 and 5 (5 = the most severe impact; 1 = the least severe).

  1   2   3   4   5

- Explain the negative effect this incident had on you at the time and in the subsequent years.

_____
_____

_____

_____

_____

_____

_____

_____

Can you now see how any or all of these incidents contributed to your negative view of yourself—your low self-esteem? This is very important in helping you see that you are not responsible for the development of your LSE—you didn't cause it—and therefore, you have nothing to be ashamed of. If you are now angry that you have had to suffer up to this point, your feelings are understandable. If you are saddened by the loss of years that you have felt paralyzed, your sadness is appropriate to the situation. Whatever your feelings, however, do not let them stand in the way of your recovery, now that you are learning what you must do.

➲   *Please go back to **Obstacle 2, "Rewriting the Script"** (page 93 in this book) and work through page 98. Instructions on page 98 will tell you where to go next.*

Obstacle 3, Excursion O

Putting This Information to Use

If you have used this workbook as it was intended, you have now put in a considerable amount of time reflecting on, remembering, and recounting your past. Much of this may have been painful, because the fact that you suffer from low self-esteem indicates that you have experienced hurtful situations in your early life. This exercise of looking at your past may have brought these experiences back to life almost as though you were facing them again. In fact, you may wonder why it was necessary to be asked to remember what you would just as soon have left dormant. You may even feel that this was a rather masochistic exercise,

Recalling the events of your past, especially the most painful ones, has been crucial to your recovery process, for hopefully it enabled you to recognize why you have low self-esteem and who contributed to its development. In doing these exercises you should now also understand that YOU ARE NOT RESPONSIBLE FOR YOUR LOW SELF-ESTEEM. *You did not choose to have low self-esteem, you did not want to have low self-esteem, you did not provide the negative information that is recorded on your videotape or in any other way create your LSE. You did not want to repeatedly sabotage your own life, and you certainly did not want to suffer as you have because of it. Instead, low self-esteem is something that others instilled in you through harsh or critical words, through abusive actions, by their absence or emotional unavailability, through neglect, or through emotional abuse such as withholding approval, affirmation, support, and expressions of love.*

If you balk at pointing the finger at someone else, remember that you have two choices: either you can admit that the words and actions of others served as the brushstrokes in painting the picture you have of yourself and from which you operate, or you can somehow think that as a small child you came up with the idea of believing in your inadequacy on your own. But how would this have been possible? Where would you have even gotten the idea that people were inadequate? How would you have come up with the concept of being unworthy or unlovable? No, everything we know we learned from our environments and the people in those *environments—we are born without* knowledge and consequently, we only know what our life—and the people in it—have taught us.

Remember that being able to determine who contributed to your LSE and how they did so does not mean you must hate that person or separate yourself from them,

Along with correctly placing the responsibility will often come an understanding of why they acted as they did, of the problems or deficiencies the person had from their own backgrounds, or that person's lack of mental health. Admitting to yourself that others are indeed culpable, does free you from the shame and guilt of believing that your LSE is something you manufactured or something that is innately wrong with you. Knowing where your LSE began and understanding that it is a learned response to negative stimuli provides comfort because what has been learned can always be relearned. In other words, since LSE isn't something you were born with but rather it is something you acquired after birth, there can be a remedy, there can be recovery.

Hopefully, you also now know from your work here and from reading ***Breaking the Chain...*** that *LSE is a serious problem*, one that isn't easily overcome. While everyone has a videotape in their head that developed following birth, the videotape of the person with LSE is negatively distorted, skewing everything he does and says. Controlled by his negativity and self-doubt, the actions of the LSE sufferer become self-defeating, thereby cementing his belief that he is inadequate, incompetent, unworthy, and unlovable. The more years that go by before the distorted tape is edited, the more convoluted the problem becomes and the more difficult it is to alter.

Thus, when people tell you that "you shouldn't feel that way" or to "just get over it," realize that it's because they don't understand what LSE really is. Many who've read ***Breaking the Chain of Low Self-Esteem*** say they didn't understand that low self-esteem was their problem or what it entailed until they read the book. Then they could see how closely it described their feelings, their behaviors, and their thinking. Instead of being angry at those well-meaning friends or family members who don't understand LSE, you might want to attempt to educate them about LSE and what it really is, especially if this person is close to you and someone who could be a support in your recovery. Explain to them why it's such a serious problem, not only for you but for all who suffer from it. Share with them why it's so difficult to overcome. Tell them you need their support, not more criticism. Go one step further and tell them what you need from them, what they could do to help you in your recovery process, because often their criticism stems from their discomfort in not knowing what to do when they see you are hurting.

Furthermore, you may now feel enraged at the people you see as responsible for your years of suffering. If so, please understand that anger is an appropriate response to this new insight. But take your time in considering how you wish to handle this new knowledge and your anger. You may decide at some point to talk to the person(s) you now know was responsible but it is usually best to wait until you are further along in your recovery before you do so, especially if you think that this person may not be receptive to your confrontation but may attempt to turn the blame back onto you. Remember too, that your goal in confronting, if you should decide to do so, is to get your anger out and to place it at the feet of those who deserve to hear it. But remember, the goal is not necessarily to make them see the error of their ways, because their responses are something you have no control over. If they are receptive, that will be wonderful, but most often this is not the case. In fact, often the perpetrator becomes defensive and tries to blame the victim, thereby heaping more coals on the fire you feel inside. In other words, while you are going through the process of recovery, the perpetrator may not be similarly enlightened or open to hearing your critical analysis of their behavior. So, be prepared for backlash when you approach these people. Be prepared to stand your ground without wavering if they do not repent or are unwilling to admit that they harmed you. Additionally, remember that if you approach them in anger, they are less likely to listen, less likely to digest what you have to say, and less likely to take any responsibility for what you say they did. Instead, your anger will give them an excuse to dismiss you as they focus on your tone rather than your message. This is not to say that you won't be angry when you talk to them, but for best results, prepare ahead of time what you wish to say, then keep your voice calm and your tone even, avoiding the use of attacking words, and using "I" statement to honestly and directly communicate your message.

You may also decide that you do not want to confront those you feel created your low self-esteem, either because you are quite certain that they will not be receptive, because they are elderly or ill and you think it serves no purpose, or because they live far away and are inaccessible. That is also a choice you have, for there is no right or wrong way to handle your feelings about your LSE. The only time it may be *necessary* for you to confront your perpetrator is when that person still plays an important and regular role in your life and where the behavior that first led to your LSE is continuing. *Under no circumstances should you submit yourself to ongoing abuse.*

Another situation to prepare yourself for is that others may push you to forgive your tormenter. Again, I say, do not rush into any such decision. Forgiveness is yours—and only yours—to give and should only be bestowed if and when you are ready. Forgiveness is not necessary for your recovery.

Hopefully you now know, on some level and some of the time, that you are not the person your mind has told you that you were all these years. And while this knowledge is crucial to your recovery, acquiring it is just one leg of the expedition that ends when you no longer or seldom suffer from LSE, when self-esteem issues are no longer interfering with your dreams and aspirations. And, now that you know that your LSE is simply a learned response to other's dysfunctional behavior, it is time to begin to alter your videotape so that it holds only information based on fact, truth, and history. Though your journey is not complete, you have made great progress in traveling toward your goal. The final piece of the expedition begins now, using the information you've attained along the way. This exercise "WHAT I'VE LEARNED ABOUT MYSELF AND MY LSE" must be performed several times a day, preferable 5 times but at least 3 times, and—for at least the next year. How rigidly you do this (and the other final exercises from Obstacle 2) over the coming months will dictate how quickly your recovery can happen. Remember, there is no short cut to overcoming LSE.

3O-1. Take the 3x5 card labeled "WHAT I'VE LEARNED ABOUT MYSELF AND MY LSE" from your packet of Self-Esteem Recovery cards.

- The card reads:
  1. I am not responsible for the development of my low self-esteem.
  2. I only came to believe what I was told and what I experienced.
  3. I have been wronged. I did not deserve to feel this way.
  4. There is nothing basically wrong with me.
  5. Knowing that I am not responsible for the development of my LSE frees me to alter it.
  6. I can change my negative thinking patterns and my self-defeating behaviors.
  7. What I don't yet know, I will learn.
  8. What I have avoided, I will face.
  9. I will base my beliefs only on fact, truth, and history.
  10. With effort and determination I will recover from low self-esteem.

- Keep this card with you at all times, in your purse or shirt pocket. (You will be writing out other cards and adding them to your collection as part of your ongoing work in overcoming Obstacle 2, until you eventually have a deck of cards that you are reading on a regular basis. Carry them all together and read each one at every opportunity.)

- Make a commitment to yourself that you will read the statements on this card 3-5 times a day—preferably 5—for the next year. Actually, this will not take a lot of your time.

- Develop some cues to remind you that it's time to read your cards, at least until reading them at set intervals becomes a habit. Such cues could be a note you place on your bathroom mirror, on the refrigerator, on the dashboard of your car, etc. Or it could be that you decide you will read the card whenever you get in your car, whenever you brush your teeth, and before or after each meal. Another strategy is to cut stars or triangles of bright construction paper and paste them in visible places as reminders—no one else need know what they are reminders of. Or you could set your watch to buzz at specific times as a reminder. You choose what cues you will set up for yourself but do try to find some method of reminding yourself it's time to read the cards. I also highly recommend that you read your cards before starting your day and before going to sleep at night.)

➲   *Please go back to **Obstacle 2, "Rewriting the Script"** (page 99 in this book) and work through page 104. Instructions on page 104 will tell you where to go next.*

Obstacle 4

Catching Up

As LSE sufferers get older, the lack of basic life skills that they failed to learn in their youth becomes more and more apparent. In adolescence, most young people experiment with forming relationships. But if a boy is too frightened to practice during those early years, he fails to develop relationship skills; then as he gets older, he is too embarrassed to try out new behaviors that others around him seem to do so skillfully. Similarly, young girls usually form close friendships with others who share information, who support them in their endeavors, and whom they can trust to be available for companionship. When a girl has had poor role models and doesn't learn how to form friendships or is so fearful of rejection that she becomes a loner, she develops a pattern that plagues her throughout life. As the years go by, these boys and girls become adult watchers who see others able to do and have the things they most want; falling further and further behind as the years go by, they feel sad and alone and are often seen by others as socially retarded or inept. Living in fear of making mistakes rather than developing their skills, they become uninteresting and unattractive with few visible attributes that would attract others.

Adult LSE sufferers may feel awkward because they lack the ability to communicate well with others on any topic below the surface level; they may not know how to start new relationships or they may be unable to maintain relationships once they're begun. Inhibited by fear and anxiety, they may not ask for what they need or express their feelings assertively. Fearful of making mistakes, they may have become followers, passively relying on others to make decisions or to initiate new experiences or they may have become aggressive and domineering people filled with anger and jealousy.

Many LSE sufferers spend these years avoiding new situations without realizing that it would be worthwhile to push themselves to walk through some of these experiences in spite of being uncomfortable. Most people expect to feel somewhat uneasy when learning a new skill or activity, but they feel the enjoyment and what they will learn far outweighs their discomfort. LSE sufferers, however, think that these new adventures are easy for everyone else; they don't recognize that their patterns of avoidance are dysfunctional, self-defeating, and the result of their low self-esteem. They don't see that they place more importance on simple mistakes, that they take things too seriously, and thus they place far more pressure on themselves than do those with healthy self-esteem. Then, because they are so tense and fearful of making a mistake or looking stupid, they are unable to relax and do their best, or sign up for a class, or participate in a new activity.

Many who suffer from severe LSE are lonely and have few friends; this is especially true of introverts. They don't belong to organizations or take part in activities outside the home, except to go to work and tend to be observers in life rather than participators. Though sad and lonely, they don't know why their lives aren't working out the way they had hoped. Too involved in protecting themselves from rejection or embarrassing moments, and too fearful of what they might see if they took a close look at themselves, they remain oblivious to how they are programming themselves for failure. Feeling unlovable they may resign themselves to a life in which they are alone and lonely, rather than try to fix what isn't working.

Extroverts with severe LSE may have many casual friends but no one who considers them special, no one to call their partner. They may be superficially involved in many activities but never really connect with any one person. They may never have gone beyond having a social or sexual relationship to one in which they could readily bare their soul with another person. Thus, some LSE sufferers may feel confused about why they can easily attract casual friends but can't convert these relationships into romantic ones.

Still others with moderate to severe low self-esteem are in relationships, even long-term relationships; many are married, but generally their relationships are rocky or at least problems exist that stem from the LSE sufferer's distorted thinking.

Many with LSE are followers who don't have anything unique to present to people; instead they are dependent on others to make the plans, chart the course of the relationship, and to define their role in the relationship. Needy and insecure, these LSE sufferers try to make friends by pleasing others and doing for others; they don't know any other way to connect with people. Then, they are disappointed when, over time, those they try to please either tire of them, deem them insignificant, or lose respect for them.

 *Before continuing, please read **Chapter 5, "Learning to Be Alone,"** (page 127-158) of **Breaking the Chain of Low Self-Esteem.***

Then return to page 271 of this book and work through page 273 where more instructions await you.

NOTE: *Unlike most books on self-esteem, this workbook zooms in on and alters the core issue of low self-esteem—your learned distorted view of self.*
Unlike most books on self-esteem, this book presents the view that the lack of basic skills in those with LSE is very important, although secondary to the real issue of directly address- ing and attacking the irrational thinking that is the foundation of LSE. LSE is the cause and poor skill development is the effect or consequence. In other words, the lack of skills is a symptom of LSE, not the main issue.
Consequently, this workbook purposely does not include long sections on skill-building. Numerous other resources provide excellent information and exercises on developing commu- nication skills, assertiveness skills, relationship skills, anger-management skills, etc.

Setting Goals

This section provides a brief overview of the various skills that LSE sufferers often fail to develop. Do not berate yourself if you realize that you fall into the category of being passive or aggressive rather than assertive or if you find yourself untrained in a specific area. Instead, realize that these are common consequences of the disorder of low self-esteem, not something you knowingly did to yourself. And remember, that just because you haven't become accomplished in a particular skill doesn't mean you can't learn it in the days ahead. Think of this as another learning experience in which you want to become aware of the aspects of your life that until now have interfered with living a happy and fulfilling life. Once you achieve this awareness, you can go about finding the resources to work on these areas of your life, thereby enhancing the likelihood of achieving your goals and dreams. Read the statements below and respond to the instructions, giving consideration to your past behavior and attitudes.

Obstacle 4, Excursion A

Work and Careers

In our work and our careers, we must, of course, have the necessary skills to perform our job well. Barring some other negative personal quality, being good at what we do generally solidifies our job standing with any company; if in addition to possessing these skills, we also work well with others, contribute new ideas, and are enthusiastic and motivated, we may be viewed as above the norm and be compensated accordingly. If not, we have the skills to move on to where our abilities are more amply rewarded.

4A-1. Think about your own work experiences. Do you feel you have made your best effort to bring to your jobs and your career the skills necessary to be successful? If not, why not? Have you advanced in your career or remained where you started? If so, why do you think this is? For example, have you needed more skills but not put forth the effort to get them? Have you talked yourself out of learning new skills because you believed you couldn't learn them or weren't motivated enough to try? Have you put forth energy and effort to get promoted? Or have you done just enough to get by? Have you stayed at a job where you weren't appropriately advanced or rewarded? If so, why have you stayed? Was it because you never considered doing anything differently? Was it because you lacked the confidence to think you could do better? Over all, explain your work history and any ways in which you think you have not achieved as much as you might have.

_____

_____

_____

_____

_____

_____

4A-2. If you became successful, explain how and why that happened. Do you think this success came naturally or do you think you became an overachiever because you have low self-esteem? Did you put yourself fully into your work in order to avoid other aspects of life in which you felt less certain that you would succeed? Did you become successful in order to prove to yourself and others that you weren't inadequate? What other reasons might explain how and why you became successful in spite of having LSE?

_____

_____

_____

_____

_____

_____

_____

If you have avoided developing a career or learning the skills necessary to seek advancement in your career, begin to formulate a plan that would include taking small steps toward that end. This may mean signing up for a class, talking to people who are presently doing what you would like to do, looking for a new job more in line with your goals, or searching the newspaper for job openings. Without a plan, you won't make any progress, so begin developing a plan today. As you continue your work of repairing your self-esteem, taking the steps that you've set out in your plan will seem more possible.

 *Please go back to **Obstacle 2, "Rewriting the Script"** (page 52 in this book) and work through page 56. Instructions on page 56 will tell you where to go next.*

Obstacle 4, Excursion B

Social Skills

To be successful both in relationships and in other parts of life, we each must have some-thing to offer that defines who we are and that distinguishes us from others—characteristics, interests, or skills that make us unique and that also cause others to be attracted to us.

Developing, and maintaining solid, satisfying relationships *with healthy people* requires that we be friendly and enjoyable to be around, that we be communicative, that we be sensitive, and that we be honest, dependable, and trustworthy. Equally important is that we be uniquely interesting. Most people with low self-esteem strive to be friend-ly; indeed they often go overboard in trying to be too nice, willingly changing their view to match that of someone who they wish to impress. They often do too much for oth-ers. This approach to developing relationships generally backfires because people lose respect for those who give too much of themselves; over-giving reveals a lack of appro-priate boundaries and self-respect. Additionally, doing too much for others is often expe-rienced as smothering and creates an unwanted sense of obligation in others.

Some who suffer from severe low self-esteem have limited lives. They go to their jobs, are quiet and withdrawn, and isolate themselves from others. Having had little practice, these people are generally poor communicators. Such LSE sufferers don't know what to say, are so fearful of saying the wrong thing, and avoid situations where they might be expected to talk to others. They seldom get into relationships unless an extrovert or another needy person takes them under their wing.

Others who have moderate to severe low self-esteem are often unpleasant to be around because they are extremely defensive, argumentative, overly sensitive, and easy to anger. If these LSE sufferers do get into relationships (while on their best behavior), they are often saddened when the relationship is short-lived due to their inconsistencies.

One of the biggest issues that plagues those with severe low self-esteem is that they may have avoided involvement in life for so long that they have become dull and uninteresting. They may be solid citizens; hard-working individuals who always play by the rules: people who are honest, dependable, and loyal, but they are boring to be around. Likely to be passive, they also tend to be dependent, somewhat rigid, and black-and-white in their thinking. They have spent their lives trying to "be good" and "playing it safe." and have often never received a traffic ticket or wouldn't think of experimenting with drugs or cheating on their taxes—not because they are so virtuous but because they are afraid of being in trouble. Too fearful to think independently, to voice their opinions, or to be creative, they are almost invisible to others. They do little to create a fun and exciting environment, almost as if they have no energy or don't know what to do. Their moods are usually flat, their demeanor reserved.

4B-1. Do you think you are friendly and enjoyable to be around? If so, why do you think this is? If not, what do you think you could do to be more friendly?

_____

_____

_____

_____

_____

_____

4B-2. Do you think you are an interesting person to be around? Do you think that people naturally gravitate to you? What makes you think this? For instance have people told you that you are really fun, exciting, or particularly interesting? What is it about you that you think others see as uniquely interesting?

_____

_____

_____

_____

_____

_____

_____

4B-3. What do you think makes anyone an interesting person? What do you find interesting about others?

_____

_____

_____

_____

_____

_____

4B-4. Think of interests you have that you would like to develop. Do you think others would see you as more interesting if you did acquire more interests?

_____

_____

_____

_____

_____

_____

4B-5. Do you see yourself as a leader or as a follower? If you are a follower most of the time, can you think of one area of your life in which you could make a special effort to lead? For example could you research new restaurants in your area, go and eat there, and then enthusiastically tell others? Or invite someone to go with you to this new place?

_____

_____

_____

_____

_____

_____

The goal concering social skills is first to become more aware of who you are, why you are the way you are, and how others may see you. The second step in developing social skills and becoming a more interesting person is to push yourself to walk through your fears, taking one small step at a time until you become more familiar and more comfortable with socializing. Continuing on your journey to overcome your self-esteem issues and the fear that accompanies it will enable you to develop more social skills.

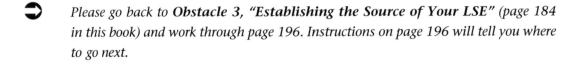

*Please go back to **Obstacle 3, "Establishing the Source of Your LSE"** (page 184 in this book) and work through page 196. Instructions on page 196 will tell you where to go next.*

Obstacle 4, Excursion C

Communication Skills

Communication is another problem for those with low self-esteem. At one extreme are those who don't even recognize their feelings and, who if they did, would feel too threatened to share them for fear of a negative reaction. Instead, they tend to communicate on a surface level, discussing mundane daily matters and other non-threatening factual information while sharing too little about themselves to arouse interest in others. If well informed, they may readily discuss impersonal issues though they will likely avoid sharing opinions about controversial issues unless they are certain the person they are addressing is in full agreement with their position.

At the other extreme are LSE sufferers who share intimate details of their lives with anyone who will listen, even total strangers. Self-focused and needy, those in this second group talk incessantly about themselves until people avoid being around them.

Additionally those with low self-esteem feel vulnerable sharing with someone how they feel about them, for fear that the feelings are not reciprocal. They have difficulty asking for what they want or need and find it hard to register a complaint about or to their significant others. People with low self-esteem tend to have unrealistic expectations and are untrusting of their partners. Therefore, they are often dissatisfied and critical. Wary that they are being used because of having been mistreated in the past, they tend to watch for signs that this is true and then unwittingly use whatever evidence they can find or conjure up to validate their doubts and to create additional ones. When they do finally communicate their displeasure the facts are distorted which both confuses and angers their partners. These irrational behaviors on the part of people with low self-esteem and the communication that follows often cause the demise of relationships.

4C-1. What are your communication patterns? For instance, are you able to share feelings? Are you comfortable when others share theirs?

_____

_____

_____

_____

_____

_____

_____

_____

4C-2. Do you avoid talking about tough issues, leaving them unresolved? Do you share your opinions or play it safe? Are you respectful of the opinions of others if they disagree with you or do you quickly get defensive?

_____

_____

_____

_____

_____

_____

4C-3. Have you ever had a Level 5 (Intimate) relationship? (refer to **Breaking the Chain**... pages 145-149) Would you like to? If you think you lack skills in how to communicate on an intimate level, what do you think you could do to learn more about this skill? Have you considered taking a class or attending a workshop on communication or relationship-building? Have you read any books on the subject? Have you considered seeing a therapist specifically to work on these issues? What are you willing to do to improve your communication skills? Just because others may not need to build their skills level in this area, doesn't mean you shouldn't or can't. Remember, there is nothing wrong with not presently having a skill—this is one of the unfortunate, negative consequences of having low self-esteem. There is something very self-defeating, however, about realizing you lack a necessary skill and not doing something about it. Make a list of what you are willing to do if you know you need help in this area.

_____

_____

_____

_____

_____

_____

➲ *Please go back to **Obstacle 3, "Establishing the Source of Your LSE"** (page 237 in this book) and work through page 255. Instructions on page 255 will tell you where to go next.*

Obstacle 4, Excursion D

Being Teachable

One of the best qualities that a person can have in life is an attitude of being teachable. The person who is teachable and open to learning from others is not usually threatened by what she doesn't know because she is confident that she can learn what she needs to. She is open to new ideas, she looks for new and more efficient ways to do things, she is willing to consider other views, and she sees the need for personal growth as a priority. The teachable person is willing to consider changing her attitudes and behaviors and is eager to improve herself.

Some people who suffer from low self-esteem fall into this category. Eager or desperate to get help, they are open and ready to charge ahead when they see a need to do so. They are highly motivated, they follow through on recovery assignments, and they are willing to expend energy to reach their goal of recovery.

Many LSE sufferers, however, are not teachable. Instead they may be extremely rigid and/or very depressed and lethargic. Some have been deeply hurt and rejected so often that they can't muster up the courage to try again with any consistency. Some are so angry and so damaged that they can't endure the thought of considering one more personal failure or inadequacy in themselves. Obviously, all of these people need a great deal of encouragement and support; they also need to experience some level of success to have any belief in a better future. One successful step can prompt a second one and the second one yet another until hopefulness is restored. The truth is that everyone needs help some of the time. However, when people who have healthy self-esteem need help or to learn something they don't know, they don't consider it a personal failure but merely something they haven't yet focused on.

Consider below how teachable you have been and what you can do to become more so.

4D-1. How teachable do you think *you* are? If you are experiencing a lack of success in any part of your life, have you been willing to consider that you may need help from other resources, e.g., books, classes, therapists, workshops, to develop more skills? If so, what have you done to follow through on that notion?

_____

_____

_____

_____

_____

4D-2. If you think you have been resistant to change, what do you think holds you back from being more teachable? Have you ever considered that being unteachable may be a problem you have?

_____

_____

_____

_____

_____

_____

4D-3. What do you think you might do differently if you were more teachable? How do you think your life might change?

_____

_____

_____

_____

_____

_____

_____

_____

➲   *Please go back to **Obstacle 2, "Rewriting the Script"** (page 89 in this book) and work through page 92. Instructions on page 92 will tell you where to go next.*

Obstacle 4, Excursion E

Learning To Be an Assertive Person

One of the skills that the majority of LSE sufferers fail to develop is assertiveness. While most people find it difficult to be consistently assertive, those with LSE find it nearly impossible, for they have learned to protect themselves by being deferential and passive or they have used anger, manipulation, and defensiveness to ward off what feels threatening. Thus, once again, the behavior patterns of those with LSE are self-defeating; although they are trying to avoid further rejection or disapproval, they deny themselves the opportunity to form healthy relationships.

Along with being assertive in relationships, of course, is the need to confront others or be confronted by them, a very frightening prospect for those with an already negative view of self. The picture in their minds is likely one of yet another person telling them they don't do things right or that they don't measure up. Or in the case of confronting another person, those with LSE often imagine a scenario in which they arouse the anger of whomever they might confront, bringing on more personal pain.

Thus, speaking the truth as they see it is always seen as potentially dangerous. Yet what's true is that living in a defensive mode where one is constantly on guard and ready to flee or deflect negative attention is in itself a painful way to live—far more painful over time than if the person learns to be assertive and experiences his strength and success in doing so.

4E-1. How assertive are you? In what areas of your life are you most assertive?

_____

_____

_____

_____

_____

_____

4E-2. Are you more likely to be passive, aggressive, passive-aggressive, or assertive? Which response mode do you use most often? Give 3 examples.

_____

_____

_____

_____

_____

_____

_____

_____

_____

_____

4E-3. If you believe that you need to increase your assertiveness, make a plan to take one small step in that direction this week. For example, decide that you are going to invite someone new to lunch, that you are going to return that item to the store that you have been putting off, or that you are going to initiate a conversation with one new person this week. Afterward, praise yourself for having accomplished what you set out to do and for being more assertive.

_____

_____

_____

_____

_____

_____

➲   *Please go back to **Obstacle 3, "Establishing the Source of Your LSE"** (page 264 in this book) and work through page 268. Instructions on page 268 will tell you where to go next.*

Obstacle 4, Excursion F

Developing New Interests

Many LSE sufferers haven't developed enough individual interests. Tending to do what others initiate or propose, they complete their routines of going to work and taking care of their homes and yards but don't find something to be passionate about that might increase their knowledge and skills, would put them in a position to meet more people, give them something unique to talk about and share with others, and help fill their time with something they really enjoy.

For instance, a person who walks might join a group that walks regularly, possibly including organized city walks. A person with an avid interest in birds might join a bird-watching group or someone who likes to play cards might join a bridge group and meet fellow players. An avid gardener might join a gardening club, or someone wanting to learn pottery-making or painting might take a class. Whatever your interests, choose one and pursue it with zest. If you find your interest increasing, the rewards will be obvious; if you decide you aren't as interested as you once thought, try something else. Trying something doesn't mean you have to stay with it for life or even for six months. Just think of it as exploring your interests and broadening your horizons.

4F-1. List interests you have but have never pursued. Don't be conservative; write down whatever comes to mind no matter how outrageous it may seem. Putting it in writing may make it seem more possible—if not now, maybe in the future.

_____

_____

_____

_____

_____

_____

4F-2. Choose one interest from your list and research it. You may find that it is something you can get involved in without too big a time or financial commitment. If you don't find any opportunities available to pursue that particularly interest you, choose another and check that one out. Decide that you are going to get involved in something that is just for you—whether or not you now know someone who is engaged in this interest.

REMEMBER:

- You are important. We must have a sense of ourselves as important, and a belief that our time and efforts are equally important.

- We must first value ourselves before others will value us.

- We must put energy into our lives and approach the future with enthusiasm.

- We must be open to growing and changing. This may mean reevaluating our beliefs, altering our view of the world.

When we have low self-esteem, we are often our own worst enemy, denying ourselves opportunities to learn, to grow, to become more interesting, to expand our views, to enjoy life. Determine as you go through the steps of recovery that you will also participate in becoming a more balanced person in every aspect of your life.

➡ *Please go forward to **Obstacle 5, "Completing the Journey"** (page 287 in this book) and work through that final section which will prepare you to continue your recovery process using your Self-Esteem Recovery Tools.*

OBSTACLE 5

Completing the Journey

Congratulations. You are nearing the end of this long leg of your journey. However, completing this workbook does not mean that your journey toward recovering from low self-esteem is finished but rather that you have equipped yourself with the necessary knowledge and skills to continue your climb toward that goal. Remember that the recovery from LSE is not quick and it is not easy, but it is achievable. So congratulations!! The fact that you are reading this paragraph most likely means that:

- You have worked hard to get here.

- You now understand how your LSE was formed and who contributed to its development.

- You have learned how your faulty thinking dictates your irrational feelings.

- You have gained a new awareness of the extent to which your emotions, and ultimately your actions and decisions, are affected by and controlled by LSE.

- You now recognize many of your patterns of self-sabotage.

- You have learned the basic steps to dismantling your LSE.

- You are hopeful about your future.

- You are as committed or more committed to recovery than when you began.

- You are ready to implement the final stage of the recovery process which is explained in the following pages.

A Map for Completing the Journey on Your Own

Hopefully, you now understand that you have within you the ability to alter and repair your low self-esteem. By now, you are able to see many of the ways in which you have been acting in self-defeating ways; more of this self-sabotage will become apparent as you go continue dismantling your distorted thinking patterns while allowing yourself only to tell yourself what is fact, truth, or based on history.

For much of the remainder of this journey, you will need to depend on yourself for the discipline to do the daily regimen that is crucial to complete recovery. You may summon help from a therapist or support person, which would be very beneficial, but you alone will be responsible for sticking to the plan, just as you are the one who will benefit if you do. Like the alcoholic who may attend AA meetings and may call a sponsor when tempted to drink, you, too, may turn to others for support. But the final decision not to drink or, in this case, not to engage in irrational thinking and self-defeating behavior, is yours alone to make.

Remember that for years you have practiced thinking in ways that are irrational and distorted, based on your fear and anxiety; remember too that fully eradicating those patterns will take time. The method of recovery that you are learning through this workbook is one that you must use regularly—preferably daily—until you feel strongly in control rather than at the mercy of your LSE. Remember too that the more diligent you are in carrying out the following instructions on a regular basis, the more inspired you will be and the greater your progress will be. Conversely, completing your daily routine haphazardly or only occasionally will most likely lead to discouragement and feelings of hopelessness.

You are encouraged to refer back to ***Breaking the Chain of Low Self-Esteem*** and this workbook as you need to. However, from this point on your personal recovery work will mainly involve the use of a notebook and 3x5 cards.

NOTE: *Beginning now, you will need to have a notebook that you dedicate to your recovery process and several packets of 3x5 cards. For your convenience, I have put together a* **Self-Esteem Recovery Toolkit**[1] *which contains the supplies you need or you may purchase a notebook and cards on your own. In addition to color-coded cards for different areas of your life, the* **Toolkit** *has additional examples and instructions for recording your experiences and for developing your* **Self-Esteem Recovery Cards** *as you continue your recovery process. When selecting a notebook on your own, consider getting one that will be convenient to carry with you.*

---

[1] Self-Esteem Recovery Toolkits and additional Self-Esteem Recovery Cards are available through www.TheSelfEsteemInstitute.com

Obstacle 5, Excursion A

Personalized Affirmations for the Self-Esteem Sufferer

5A-1. Look at each of the statements below. If you agree with one, copy it on a 3x5 card and carry this card with you at all times. Those statements you don't agree with, you should not include on your card. Therefore, examine each statement for truth, fact, and your own personal history before deciding to add it or to omit it. Once you have decided what to include on your card, read the statements to yourself at least 5 times throughout the day until you have them memorized. Continue repeating them 3-5 times a day for a period of 3-6 months.

NOTE: *Unlike most books on affirmations, this book encourages you to only use affirmations that speak to you personally. This generalized grouping of affirmations is recommended because they have proven to ring true for most people who suffer from LSE and who have completed this journey, whether through this workbook or through therapy.*

- There is nothing basically wrong with me. I am worthy, deserving, and lovable.

- LSE has caused my negative view of self, which is both irrational and untrue.

- The words, actions, and attitudes of others have created my LSE. I am not to blame.

- I acquired LSE through no fault of my own; therefore, I don't need to be ashamed.

- I will make a conscious effort to no longer allow fear to be the motivating factor in my life.

- Fear and anxiety have prompted me to continually perform self-defeating behaviors. Now that I recognize this, I can alter these patterns of self-sabotage.

- I can learn the skills I now lack and have avoided learning because of fear.

- I am committed to recovering from my LSE and, like a soldier with a mission, will continue to fight the battle.

- I will not expect others to understand what I struggle with or why I act as I do. However, I can educate them if I wish to do so.

- Good mental health is within my grasp, if I'm willing to work for it.

Obstacle 5, Excursion B

How to Use Your Notebook

Plan to use your notebook every day. In the morning write the date at the top of a new page and whenever possible, carry the notebook with you. During the day or at least in the evening, record any upsetting or anxious events from the day. For instance, if you had a disagreement with someone that provoked a self-esteem attack at the time or later, write this down. Or if you became upset because someone didn't return your phone call or cancelled plans with you, jot this in your notebook. It is best, of course, to have your notebook with you at all times so that you won't forget any of these incidents, but if that is not possible, set aside time after work or following dinner to document the events of your day and to work through the steps below. Waiting until bedtime is usually counter-productive as you are tired, less alert, and less motivated than earlier in the day.

5B-1. As you write down the details of your day, use one page for each incident, allowing room below the incident for the next step of the process. Be sure to note who was involved, what was said or not said, what was done or not done. For instance, you might write, "While at lunch with three of my coworkers, I spilled soup down the front of my pink silk blouse. Everyone oohed and ahhed sympathetically but I saw Pearl roll her eyes at Stephanie as if to say, 'What a slob.'"

5B-2. While it is your goal to isolate the specific things you said to yourself at the time of the incident, things that led to your negative feelings, it may be necessary to first describe your feelings. This may help you backtrack to the self-statements you were saying, since we know that *feelings are the result of thinking*. Therefore, below your description of the negative incident, jot down the feelings you experienced immediately after and later on following this specific incident.

5B-3. Next write down the specific statements you think you said to yourself at the time of the incident. Don't be embarrassed to write these statements down as they are typical of all people who have low self-esteem, not something that you alone do. For instance, when you spilled the soup, did you say to yourself, "They probably think I'm a slob" or "I saw Pearl roll her eyes at Stephanie—they must think I'm ridiculous" or "I can't believe I did that. What's wrong with me?" or "I never do anything right" or "If I don't stop doing these dumb things, they will quit inviting me to join them for lunch." Write down as many of these statements as you can think of or that you imagine you might have said.

Now put these self-statements in the order of magnitude. Typically, when people with LSE berate themselves, they do so by starting with one simple incident and then adding self-statements that increase in scope and severity as they go along. For instance, in the incident above (spilling the soup), the self-statements moved from a) what others think (that I'm a slob or ridiculous) to b) the possible long range consequences (they will quit inviting me to lunch), to c) broad implications like "what's *wrong* with me" or condemning statements like "I *never* do anything right." Thus, instead of saying "I made a mistake," you say "There is something innately *wrong* with me," or "I will *never* get it right." In other words, people with low self-esteem become more irrational once they start berating themselves. Each successive statement builds upon the irrationality of the one before it, decreasing its factual content and increasing the depth of self-loathing, depression, and hopelessness the LSE sufferer experiences.

Obstacle 5, Excursion C

Using the Self-Esteem Recovery Cards

Use one card for each incident you write in your notebook. You are advised to write a card each time you get upset due to your LSE (whenever you overreact, get your feelings hurt, feel rejected, think others are mistreating you, question whether others are trustworthy, feel other don't like you, are too fearful to participate in an activity, feel you have done something inappropriate or embarrassed yourself, etc.)

5C-1. Give each card a title and write that title at the top of the card along with the date that you are writing it. For instance, in the example above your title might simply be "spilling soup" or "lunch with coworkers" or "embarrassing myself while with coworkers." Thus, the title is composed of a few words that will help remind you of the incident. You can also put a title on the card such as "Work issues" if the incident is about specific issues related only to work.

5C-2. Taking each irrational statement that you have written in your notebook for your first incident, alter the statement so that it is based on truth, fact, or history. For instance, true statements in this situation might include "I was embarrassed when I spilled my soup, but accidents happen to everyone" or "I felt bad about spilling soup on my silk blouse but it can be cleaned" or "My friends felt bad for me and probably were thinking they were glad it wasn't them" or "Everybody makes mistakes at times. Today was just my day" or "My coworkers are nice women and understand that these things just happen" or "Spilling food at a meal doesn't mean anything about the kind of person I am—everyone makes mistakes."

NOTE: *If you have difficulty constructing statements that are true, rational, and factual, you may need to ask your support person for help. (The author, Dr. Sorensen is available for phone consultation if you need her assistance.* Email her at mjsorensen@TheSelfEsteemInstitute.com for details).

5C-3. Carry this card with you at all times. Find 5 or more opportunities each day to read your cards. Read them one or more times at each sitting. Read them out loud when possible. Read them with conviction. Concentrate on the content of each statement as you say them. (You may want to read these cards while brushing your teeth in the mornings or while eating breakfast, when stopped at a stop light while commuting to and from work, at your desk at work since it only takes a few minutes, in the restroom where no one will see you, during your morning or afternoon break, taking a walk at lunchtime, taking a bath, fixing dinner, etc.

5C-4. Reading your cards first thing in the morning will help start your day off right. Reading them before going to sleep will help lower your anxiety and enhance your rest.

5C-5. You may want to write these statements in your notebook as well as on your cards. Then, if a card should ever be lost, you can write out a new one. If you are concerned that someone might find your cards, don't put your name on them; then if someone does read them, they won't know the cards belong to you.

5C-6. If someone sees you reading your cards and asks you what you are doing, remember that you don't ever have to tell anyone anything you don't want to. Instead, you can just say, "The cards are just a list of things I'm trying to remember" or "They are part of a self-growth project I'm working on" or "It's just a personal project I'm working on." You don't have to say, "Well, I have low self-esteem and I'm trying to overcome it," though that would be perfectly fine to say if you knew the person well, trusted them, and had decided to confide in them.

5C-7. Feel free to retire a card:
- when you think that you have overcome the particular issue it addresses
- if you have the card so well memorized that you can now say it without thinking,
- when for any other reason it no longer seems applicable.

5C-8. Use your cards consciously with the expectation that positive change will occur. Don't allow yourself to get into a pattern of begrudgingly and haphazardly using your cards, which would be another self-sabotage, then telling yourself the method just doesn't work.

Obstacle 5, Excursion D

How to Most Effectively Use the Self-Esteem Recovery Cards

Hundreds of people have overcome their low self-esteem through this proven method. For best results, develop a regimented program for when you are going to read your cards. Five times a day is suggested, allowing 5-10 minutes each time, though some people use them for much longer periods of time, repeating the statements when commuting, waiting in the doctor's office, or standing in line. Some set their watches to buzz so that they read their cards regularly throughout the day; others religiously read their cards before or after meals. Devise your own strategy, but do make a plan. If you leave it to chance and are unscheduled, it won't happen often enough to be helpful—especially after the first week or two. For the cards to be effective, do the following:

5D-1. CARRY YOUR CARDS WITH YOU AT ALL TIMES.

5D-2. MAKE A CONCRETE PLAN TO USE ALL OF YOUR CARDS 5 TIMES A DAY, EVERY DAY.

5D-3. In addition, WHENEVER AN INCIDENT OCCURS that is similar to one or more of your existing cards, use that as a signal to read all of your cards.

5D-4. MAKE TIME AS SOON AS POSSIBLE AFTER YOU HAVE EXPERIENCED A NEW INCIDENT (A SELF-ESTEEM ATTACK) TO WRITE A NEW CARD. Each evening, review your day and write a card for any incident that occurred that day that you did not have time to address during the day.

5D-5. BE SURE THE STATEMENTS YOU WRITE ON YOUR RECOVERY CARDS ARE ACCURATE AND BASED ON FACT, TRUTH, AND HISTORY. If your cards are negative or inaccurate instead, recovery will be sidetracked.

5D-6. GET HELP IF YOU HAVE DIFFICULTY FIGURING OUT HOW YOUR SELF-STATEMENTS ARE IRRATIONAL AND HOW THEY CAN BE RESTATED. You will likely need support as you go through this process. Ask your partner, a close friend, or a therapist to help you. Discuss this, however, only with people who care about you, who are sensitive to your feelings, and who are supportive of your work.

5D-7. DON'T EVALUATE YOUR PROGRESS EVERY DAY. Progress generally doesn't occur immediately. Often, people do not see their own progress very well and need someone to point it out to them. In fact, it may take weeks before you start to see the difference this recovery program is making in your life—and then this will occur only if you have been diligent in working the program consistently. Remember that you have practiced telling yourself irrational and inaccurate information hundreds of times a day for years. To counter the damage done will take time and perseverance—but recovery is a certainty if you fully do the work of recognizing and replacing negative, irrational self-talk with positive or neutral, rational self-statements on a consistent basis.

5D-8. GO FOR IT! RECOVERY IS NOW UP TO YOU! Commit yourself to a year of dedication to this process and your life will never be the same.

Don't be discouraged that there is more to do. Remember you can now make a choice to either focus on the fact that you aren't finished or be encouraged by the reality that you have come a long way in your journey toward recovery and that you now possess the awareness, knowledge, and the tools to move ahead. Remember that anything worth having is worth working for, so keep your chin up, your eyes on the road ahead, and your commitment unwavering. Happy Traveling!

A note from the author:

Please feel free to email me at mjsorensen@TheSelfEsteemInstitute.com with your comments. I read all of my emails, though I don't read lengthy ones in their entirety. I welcome your comments, but please remember that I get many, and limit your writing to 2-3 short paragraphs. I respond to all emails that are of an appropriate nature and when I am in town, try to do so within 48 hours.

If you want feedback or suggestions for recovery, I offer phone consultation and therapy to people across the country and email therapy to those outside the U.S. If you are interested in these services, please ask for information on fees and how the process works.

(Students, please do not email me if you want me to provide you with information for your papers, to suggest research topics, or to do your research for you. I recommend instead, that you read my books.)

To order additional copies:
1. Go to my website: www.TheSelfEsteemInstitute.com where discounts are offered on all books and where information is available on how to make credit card purchases.
2. Or order through the mail by sending a check for $22.95 (free shipping) to Wolf Publishing Co., 16890 SW Daffodil St., Sherwood, OR 97140

Large quantity discounts are available.
Call 503-293-6608 or email Dr. Sorensen for details.